the *studies in* the Sermon on the Mount

# studies in the Sermon on the Mount

God's Character and the Believer's Conduct

# Oswald Chambers

Discovery House.
from Our Daily Bread Ministries

*Studies in the Sermon on the Mount:*
*God's Character and the Believer's Conduct*

© 1960 by Oswald Chambers Publications Association Limited

This updated language edition © 2016
by Oswald Chambers Publications Association Limited

Discovery House is affiliated with Our Daily Bread Ministries,
Grand Rapids, Michigan.

Requests for permission to quote from this book should be directed to:
Permissions Department, Discovery House, P.O. Box 3566,
Grand Rapids, MI 49501, or contact us by e-mail at
permissionsdept@dhp.org.

All Scripture quotations, unless otherwise indicated, are from
the New King James Version®. Copyright © 1982 by Thomas Nelson.
Used by permission. All rights reserved.

Scripture quotations marked KJV are from the King James Version.

ISBN: 978-1-62707-498-8

*Printed in the United States of America*

Second printing of this edition in 2016

# Contents

# Publisher's Foreword

These Bible studies on Matthew 5–7 were first given by Oswald Chambers at the League of Prayer's annual summer convention in Perth, Scotland, in July 1911. They were published as articles in 1912, and as a book in 1915 by God's Bible School, in Cincinnati, Ohio. A favorite among all his writings, they serve to enlarge our understanding of Jesus' teaching on what His life in us really means in terms of its outworking in the believer's experience.

For Chambers, the Christian life is authenticated when the indwelling Spirit applies the principles of Christ to the particular circumstances in which the believer is placed. This is doctrine in work clothes, truth become reality, redemption expressed. And, consistent with all of his writings, the author reminds us in these studies that our focus must be on God alone and not on those among whom we live.

We are pleased to release this newly edited, updated-language edition of *Studies in the Sermon on the Mount* as part of the Oswald Chambers Library.[1] It is our hope that this book will fuel the reader's passion to know and love Jesus Christ, the living Word, and further his or her appreciation for the teaching of God's written Word and the application of its truth in all of life.

THE PUBLISHER

---

1. The complete, original text of *Studies in the Sermon on the Mount* is available in *The Complete Works of Oswald Chambers* (Discovery House).

# Chapter One

# His Teaching and Our Training
## *Matthew 5:1–20*

To understand the Sermon on the Mount, it is necessary to have the mind of its preacher, Jesus himself—and this knowledge can be gained by anyone who will receive the Holy Spirit (see Luke 11:13; John 20:22; Acts 19:2–6). The Spirit alone can expound the teachings of Jesus Christ.

There is one abiding method of interpreting the teachings of Jesus: it is the Spirit of Jesus in the heart of the believer, applying Jesus' principles to the particular circumstances in which the believer is placed. "Be transformed by the renewing of your mind," says the apostle Paul, "that you may prove [that is, grasp the meaning of] what is that good and acceptable and perfect will of God" (Romans 12:2).

Beware of placing our Lord's role as *teacher* ahead of His purpose as *savior*. That tendency is prevalent today, and it is dangerous. We must know Jesus first as savior before His teaching can have any meaning for us—or, we could say, before it can have any meaning other than that of an ideal which leads to despair. Imagine coming to men and women of defective lives and defiled hearts and telling them to be pure in heart! What is the use of giving us an ideal we cannot possibly attain? We are happier without it.

If Jesus is only a teacher, all He can do is tantalize us by erecting a standard we cannot come anywhere near. But if—by being born again from above—we know Him first as savior, we know that He did not come only to teach us: *He came to make us what He teaches we should be.* The Sermon on the Mount is a statement of the life we *will* live when the Holy Spirit is having His way with us.

The Sermon on the Mount produces despair in the heart of an unsaved person, and that is the very thing Jesus means it to do—because as soon as we reach the point of despair we are willing to come to Him as paupers to receive from Him. "Blessed are the poor in spirit"—that is the first principle of the kingdom. As long as we have a conceited, self-righteous idea that we can do these things if God will help us, God allows us to go on until we break the neck of our ignorance over some obstacle. Then we will be willing to come and receive from Him.

The bedrock of Jesus Christ's kingdom is poverty, not possession. It is not "decisions for Jesus Christ," but a sense of absolute futility: "I cannot begin to do it." Then, says Jesus, you are blessed. It takes us a long while to believe we are poor, but that is the entrance. The knowledge of our own poverty brings us to the moral frontier where Jesus Christ works.

Every mind has two compartments, the conscious and subconscious. We say that many of the things we hear and read slip away from memory; they don't really, they simply pass into the subconscious mind. It is the Holy Spirit's work to bring back to our conscious minds the things that are stored in the subconscious. When studying the Bible, never think that if you do not understand it, it is of no use. A particular truth may be of no use to you just now—but when circumstances arise in which that truth is needed, the Holy Spirit will bring it to your remembrance.

This accounts for the surprising emergence of Jesus' words in our minds. We say, "I wonder where that came from?" But Jesus said that the Holy Spirit would "bring to your remembrance all things that I said to you" (John 14:26). The real question is this: Will I obey Him when He does bring it to my remembrance? If I discuss the matter with someone else, the probability is that I will *not* obey. The apostle Paul said, "I did not immediately confer with flesh and blood" (Galatians 1:16). Always trust the originality of the Holy Spirit when He brings a word to your remembrance.

Always remember the twofold aspect of the mind—there is nothing supernatural or mysterious about it, it is simply the knowledge of how God has made us. To judge yourself only by what you consciously understand at a certain time would be foolish. There may be many things of which you do not grasp the meaning—but as you go on storing Bible truth in your mind, the Holy Spirit will bring back to your conscious mind the word you need and apply it to your particular circumstances. These three things always work together—moral intelligence, the spontaneous originality of the Holy Spirit, and the time and place of a life lived in communion with God.

## Divine Disproportion

*(Matthew 5:1–12)*

Our Lord began His discourse by saying, "Blessed are . . . ," and His hearers must have been staggered by what followed. According to Jesus Christ, they were to be blessed in every condition which they had been taught—from earliest childhood—to regard as a curse. Our Lord was speaking to Jews, and they believed that the sign of God's blessing was material prosperity in every shape and form. Yet Jesus said people are blessed for exactly the opposite: "Blessed are the poor in spirit. . . . Blessed are those who mourn," and so on.

### The "Mines" of God • Matthew 5:1–10; compare to Luke 6:20–26

The first time we read the Beatitudes, they appear to be simple and beautiful statements, not at all startling; they go unobserved into the subconscious mind. We are so used to the sayings of Jesus that they slip past us; they sound sweet and pious and wonderfully simple, but they are in reality like spiritual torpedoes that burst and explode in the subconscious mind. When the Holy Spirit brings them back to our conscious minds, we realize what startling statements they are.

For instance, the Beatitudes seem to be merely mild and beautiful principles for otherworldly people, of very little use for the stern world in which we live. We soon find, however, that they contain the dynamite of the Holy Spirit. They explode like "spiritual mines" when our circumstances require them to do so. They rip and tear and revolutionize all our ideas of life.

When the light of these truths is brought to the conscious mind, the test of discipleship is obedience. We do not hunt through the Bible for some precept to obey—Jesus' teaching never leads us to moral snobbery and arrogance. Instead, we should live so in touch with God that the Holy Spirit can continually call up some word of His and apply it to our circumstances. We are not tested until the Holy Spirit brings the word back.

We are not called to apply the Beatitudes literally, but to allow the life of God to invade us by regeneration, and then to soak our minds in the teaching of Jesus Christ. This teaching will slip down into the subconscious mind, and at some point, circumstances will arise in which one of Jesus Christ's statements emerges. Instantly, we must decide whether we will accept the tremendous spiritual revolution that will be produced if we obey this precept of His.

If we do obey, our actual life will become different—we will find we have the power to obey if we choose. That is the way the Holy Spirit works in the heart of a disciple. (And remember that our Lord's teaching applies only to those who are His disciples.) To begin with, the teaching of Jesus Christ comes with astonishing discomfort, because it is out of all proportion to our natural way of looking at things. But Jesus puts in a new sense of proportion, and slowly we form our way of life on the line of His precepts.

## The Motive of Godliness • Matthew 5:11–12

The motive that underlies the precepts of the Sermon on the Mount is love of God. Read the Beatitudes with your mind fixed on God, and you will realize their neglected side.

Their meaning in relationship to people is so obvious that it scarcely needs stating, but the aspect toward God is not so obvious.

"Blessed are the poor in spirit"—toward God. Am I a pauper toward God? Do I know that I cannot prevail in prayer, I cannot blot out the sins of the past, I cannot alter my disposition, I cannot lift myself nearer to God? Then I am in the one place where I am able to receive the Holy Spirit. People cannot receive the Holy Spirit until they are convinced of their own spiritual poverty.

"Blessed are the meek"—toward God's commands and promises.

"Blessed are the merciful"—to God's reputation. When I am in trouble, do I awaken sympathy for myself? Then I slander God, because the reflexive thought in people's minds is, "How hard God is with that person!" It is easy to slander God's character because He never attempts to vindicate himself.

"Blessed are the pure in heart"—that is obviously Godward.

"Blessed are the peacemakers"—making peace between God and man, the note that was struck at the birth of Jesus.

Is it possible to live out the Beatitudes? Never—unless God can do what Jesus Christ says He can; unless He can give us the Holy Spirit, who will remake us and bear us into a new realm. The essential element in the saint's life is simplicity, and Jesus Christ makes the motive of godliness gloriously simple—that is, be carefully careless about everything except your relationship to Him.

The motive of a disciple is to be pleasing to God. The true happiness of the saint is found in purposefully making and keeping God first. Here is the great difference between Jesus Christ's principles and all other moral teaching: Jesus bases everything on *God*-realization, while others focus on *self*-realization.

There is a difference between devotion to principles and devotion to a person. Jesus Christ never proclaimed a cause, He proclaimed personal devotion to himself: *"for My sake."* Discipleship is not based on devotion to abstract ideals, but on devotion to the Lord Jesus Christ, so the whole of the Christian life is stamped by originality.

Whenever the Holy Spirit sees a chance to glorify Jesus Christ, He will take your whole personality and make it blaze and glow with a passionate devotion to the Lord Jesus. You are no longer the devotee of a cause or principle—you are the committed, loving slave of the Lord Jesus. No person on earth has that love unless the Holy Ghost has imparted it. People may admire Jesus, and respect Him, and reverence Him—but we cannot *love* God until the Holy Spirit has "poured out" that love in our hearts (Romans

5:5). The only true lover of the Lord Jesus Christ is the Holy Spirit.

> *"Blessed are you when they revile and persecute you, and say all kinds of evil against you falsely for My sake."*

Jesus Christ says that blessedness—high goodness and rare happiness—comes from suffering "for My sake." It is not suffering for conscience' sake or for conviction's sake or because of the ordinary troubles of life, but something beyond all that: "for My sake."

"Blessed are you when men hate you, and when they exclude you, and revile you, and cast out your name as evil, for the Son of Man's sake" (Luke 6:22). Jesus did not say, "Rejoice when men separate you from their company because of your own crotchety notions," but when they criticize you, *"for My sake."* When you begin to conduct yourself among others as a saint, you will stand absolutely alone—you will be reviled and persecuted. No one can stand that unless he or she is in love with Jesus Christ. You cannot stand that treatment for a conviction or creed, but you can do it for a Being you love.

Devotion to a Person is the only thing that tells—devotion to the death to a *Person,* not to a creed or doctrine.

# Divine Disadvantage

*(Matthew 5:13–16)*

In today's world, the saints' disadvantage is that their confession of Jesus Christ is not to be secret, but glaringly public. It would certainly be to our advantage, from the standpoint of self-fulfillment, to keep quiet. And, nowadays, there is a growing tendency to say, "Be a Christian, live a holy life; just don't talk about it."

Our Lord uses as illustrations some of the most conspicuous things known to humanity: salt, light, and a city set on a hill. He says, essentially, "Be like *that* in your home, your business, your church. Be a conspicuous Christian, ready for either ridicule or respect depending upon the people you are with."

Later, in Matthew 10:26–28, our Lord again taught the need to be bold proclaimers of the truth. We are not to cover it up for fear of wolfish people.

## Concentrated Service • Matthew 5:13

Not *consecrated* service, but *concentrated*. Consecration (our dedication) would soon become sanctification (holiness) if we would only concentrate on what God wants. Concentration means pinning down the four corners of the mind until it is settled on what God wants. The literal interpretation of the Sermon on the Mount is child's play; its interpretation by the Holy Spirit is the hard work of a saint, and it requires spiritual concentration.

"You are the salt of the earth." Some teachers today seem to think our Lord said, "You are the *sugar* of the earth," meaning the ideal of the Christian is gentleness and winsomeness without any curative discomfort. But our Lord's illustration of a Christian is *salt,* one of the most concentrated things we know, something that preserves wholesomeness and prevents decay.

It is a disadvantage to be salt. Think of the action of salt on a wound, and you will realize this. If you get salt into a wound, it hurts—and when God's children are among those who are "raw" toward God, their presence causes discomfort. The man who is wrong with God is like an open wound, and when "salt" gets into him, it causes annoyance and distress— he becomes spiteful and bitter. The disciples of Jesus today preserve society from corruption; the "salt" of their presence causes irritation, which leads to their persecution.

How are we to maintain the healthy, salty tang of saintliness? By keeping our right relationship to God through Jesus Christ. In this present age, Jesus says, "The kingdom of God does not come with observation. . . . For, indeed, the kingdom of God is within you" (Luke 17:19, 21). Christians are called to live out Jesus' teaching in a culture that will not recognize Him, and that spells resistance and very often persecution.

This is the day of the humiliation of the saints. The next dispensation will be the glorification of the saints, when the kingdom of God will be outside as well as inside men.

## Conspicuous Setting • Matthew 5:14–16

The illustrations our Lord uses are all conspicuous: salt, light, and a city on a hill. There is no possibility of mistaking them. To preserve something from corruption, salt has to be placed in the midst of it. Before it can do its work, it causes excessive irritation—which leads to persecution. Light attracts moths and bats, and points out the way for burglars as well as honest people. A city is a gathering place for all the human driftwood that will not work for its own living, and a Christian will have any number of parasites and ungrateful hangers-on. Jesus would have us remember that other people will certainly defraud us. These considerations form a powerful temptation: we may want to pretend we are not salt, to put our light under a bushel basket, and to cover our city with a fog. But Jesus allows nothing in the nature of covert discipleship.

"You are the light of the world." Light cannot be soiled; you may reach for a beam of light with the dirtiest hand, but you leave no mark on it. A sunbeam may shine into the filthiest home in the slum of a city, but it will not be soiled. Merely moral people may be soiled in spite of their integrity, but those who are made pure by the Holy Spirit cannot be soiled—they are as light.

Thank God for those men and women who spend their lives in the slums of the earth, not as social reformers to lift their brothers and sisters to cleaner sties, but as the light of God, revealing a way back to Him. God keeps these workers as the light, pure and undefiled. If you have been covering your light, uncover it! Walk as children of light. People may dislike it, preferring darkness when their deeds are evil— but the light reveals sin and guides to a better way (John 3:19–21).

Are we the salt of the earth? Are we the light of the world? Are we allowing God to exhibit in our lives the truth of these startling statements of Jesus Christ?

# Divine Declaration
*(Matthew 5:17–20)*

### His Mission • Matthew 5:17–19
*"I came . . . to fulfill."*

What an amazing statement! When we hear Jesus Christ speak, we should remove our shoes as if we are standing on holy ground, and strip every careless, commonsense attitude from our minds. In Jesus, we deal with God as man, the

God-Man, the representative of the whole human race in one Person. The men of His day traced their religious pedigree back to the nature of God, and this young Nazarene carpenter said, "*I am* the nature of God." So to them He was blasphemous.

Our Lord makes himself the exact meaning and fulfillment of all Old Testament prophecy. His mission, He says, is to fulfill the Law and the Prophets. He further says that any person who breaks the old laws (because they belong to a former dispensation) and teaches other people to break them as well, will suffer severe impoverishment.

If the old commandments were difficult, our Lord's principles are unbelievably more difficult. Everything He teaches is impossible unless He can put into us His Spirit and remake us from within. The Sermon on the Mount is quite unlike the Ten Commandments in the sense of its being absolutely unworkable—unless Jesus Christ can remake us.

There are teachers who argue that the Sermon on the Mount supersedes the Ten Commandments, and that—"because we are not under law but under grace" (Romans 6:15)—it does not matter whether we honor our father and mother, whether we covet, or so on. Beware of statements like this: "There is no need nowadays to observe giving a tenth either of money or time; we are in a new dispensation and everything belongs to God." That, in practical application, is sentimental dust-throwing. The giving of the tenth is not a sign that all belongs to God, but a sign that the tenth belongs to God and the rest is ours—and we are held responsible for what we do with it.

To be "not under law but under grace" does not mean that we can do as we like. It is surprising how easily we can wriggle out of Jesus Christ's principles by one or two pious sayings repeated often. The only safeguard against this is to keep personally related to God. The secret of all spiritual understanding is to walk in the light—not the light of our convictions or our own theories, but the light of God (1 John 1:7).

### His Message • Matthew 5:20

Think of the most upright person you know who has never received the Holy Spirit. Think of the most moral, sterling, religious person, such as Nicodemus or his fellow Pharisee Saul of Tarsus, who was called "blameless" according to the law (Philippians 3:6). Jesus says you must exceed that person in righteousness. You have to be not only as moral as the most moral human being you know, but infinitely more—to be so right in your actions, so pure in your motives, that almighty God can see nothing to blame in you.

Is it too strong to call this a spiritual torpedo? These statements of Jesus are the most revolutionary statements human ears ever heard, and we need the Holy Spirit to interpret them to us. Today's shallow admiration for "Jesus Christ as a teacher" is of no use.

Who is going to climb that "hill of the Lord" (Psalm 24:3)? To stand before God and say, as Psalm 24:4 indicates, "My hands are clean, my heart is pure"? Who can do that? Who can stand in the eternal light of God and have nothing at all for God to blame? Only the Son of God. Then if the Son of God is formed in us by regeneration and sanctification, He will exhibit himself through our lives on earth. That is the ideal of Christianity—"that the life of Jesus also may be manifested in our mortal flesh" (2 Corinthians 4:11).

Jesus says our inclinations must be right to their depths, not only our conscious motives but also our unconscious ones. Now we are beyond our own abilities. Can God make me pure in heart? Blessed be His name, He can! Can He alter my disposition so that when circumstances reveal me to myself, I am amazed? He can. Can He impart His nature to me until it is identically the same as His own? He can. That, and nothing less, is the meaning of His cross and resurrection.

"Unless your righteousness *exceeds* . . ." The righteousness of the scribes and Pharisees was right, not wrong. Of course, they did things that were not righteous, but Jesus is speaking here of their *righteousness,* which His disciples are to exceed. What exceeds right *doing*? Is it not the addition of right *being*? Right being without right doing is possible if we refuse to enter into relationship with God, but that cannot exceed "the righteousness of the scribes and Pharisees." Jesus Christ's message here is that our righteousness must exceed that of the scribes and Pharisees, who were very good at *doing*, though they were nothing in *being*. Otherwise, we will never enter into the kingdom of heaven.

Monks in the Middle Ages refused to take the responsibilities of life and shut themselves away from the world; all they wanted was the *being*. Many people today want to do the same thing, and cut themselves off from one relationship or another. But that does not exceed the righteousness of the scribes and Pharisees. If our Lord had meant exceed in *being* only, He would not have used the word *exceed*—He would have said, "Except your righteousness *be otherwise than . . .*" We cannot exceed the righteousness of the most moral people we know on the line of what they *do,* but only on the line of what they *are.*

The teaching of the Sermon on the Mount must produce despair in the unsaved person; if it does not, it is because he or she has paid no attention to it. When you do pay attention to Jesus Christ's teaching, you will soon say, like the apostle Paul, "Who is sufficient for these things?" (2 Corinthians 2:16). The answer is this: "Blessed are the pure in heart." If Jesus Christ means what He says, where do we stand? "Come to Me," He says (Matthew 11:28).

# Chapter Two

# Actual and Real
## *Matthew 5:21–42*

A person cannot take in anything that he or she has not begun to think about—so until people are born again, what Jesus says does not mean anything to them. The Bible is a universe of revealed facts that have no meaning for us until we are born from above. When we are born again, we see in the Bible what we never saw before. We are lifted to the realm where Jesus lives, and we begin to see what He sees (John 3:3).

By *actual* I mean the things we come in contact with by our senses. By *real* I mean those things which lie behind, things we cannot get at by our senses (2 Corinthians 4:18). Fanatics see only the real and ignore the actual; materialists look at the actual only, and ignore the real. The only sane

Being who ever walked this earth was Jesus Christ, because in Him the actual and the real were one.

Jesus Christ does not stand first in the actual world, He stands first in the real world. That is why the natural person does not bother about Jesus—"the natural man does not receive the things of the Spirit of God, for they are foolishness to him" (1 Corinthians 2:14).

When we are born from above we begin to see actual things in the light of the real. We say that prayer changes things, but prayer does not change actual things nearly so much as it changes the person who sees the actual things. In the Sermon on the Mount our Lord brings the actual and the real together.

## The Account with Purity

*(Matthew 5:21–30)*

Our Lord in these verses is laying down the principle that if people are going to follow Him and obey His Spirit, they must make up their mind to be pure. We can't make ourselves pure by obeying laws. Purity is not a question of doing things right, but of the doer *being* right on the inside.

Purity is difficult to define. But we can think of it as a state of heart just like the heart of our Lord Jesus Christ. Purity is not innocence—innocence is the characteristic of a child, and though in profound ways a child is not pure, her innocence presents us with all that we understand by purity. Innocence in a child's life is a beautiful thing, but men and women ought not to be innocent—they should be tested and tried and pure.

No one is born pure; purity is the outcome of conflict. The pure person is not the one who has never been tried, but the one who knows what evil is and has overcome it. (The same is true of virtue and morality—no one is born virtuous and moral, we are born without moral perception. Our morality is always the outcome of conflict, not something that arises automatically within us.)

Jesus Christ demands that our purity be explicit as well as implicit—that is, my actual conduct, the actual chastity of my bodily life, the actual chastity of my mind, is to be beyond the condemnation of almighty God. We are not to be pure beyond the condemnation of fellow humans, since that could turn us into Pharisees. We can always deceive other people.

But Jesus Christ has taken upon himself, by His redemption, to put in me a heart that is so pure that God can see nothing in it to criticize. That is the marvel of the redemption—that Jesus Christ can give me a new heredity, the unsullied heredity of the Holy Spirit. If it is there, Jesus says, his purity will work out in my actual experience.

In Matthew 15, our Lord tells His disciples what the human heart is like. "Out of the heart come . . ." (verse 19), and then follows the ugly list: murder, adultery, theft, and so on. We may say, "I never felt any of those things in my heart," preferring to trust our innocent ignorance rather than Jesus Christ's penetrating wisdom. Either Jesus Christ is not worth listening to, or He must be the supreme authority on the human heart.

So if I make *conscious* innocence the test, I am likely to come to a place where I find—with a shuddering realization—that what Jesus said is true, and I will be appalled at the possibility of evil inside me. If I have never been outwardly vile, the reason is probably a mixture of cowardice and the protection of civilized life. But when I am undressed before God, I find that Jesus Christ is right in His diagnosis. As long as I remain under the refuge of innocent ignorance, I am living in a fool's paradise. There is always guilt to be found in myself when I try to disprove what Jesus says.

Jesus Christ demands that the heart of a disciple be utterly pure, and unless He can give me His disposition, His teaching simply teases me. If all He came to do was mock me by telling me to be what I know I never can be, I can afford to ignore Him. But if Jesus can give me His own disposition of holiness, then I begin to see how I can actually be pure. Jesus Christ is both the sternest and the gentlest of saviors.

The good news of God is not only that Jesus died for my sins, but that He gave himself for me that I might give myself to Him. God cannot accept goodness from me, He can only accept my badness—and He will give me the solid goodness of the Lord Jesus in exchange (see 2 Corinthians 5:21).

## Disposition and Deeds • Matthew 5:21–22

Our Lord is using an illustration that was familiar to the disciples. If a man disregarded proper public behavior, he was in danger of being brought to a court, and if he was contemptuous with that court, he was in danger of the final judgment. Jesus uses this illustration of the ordinary exercise of judgment to show what the attitude of a disciple must be like—that my motives, which arise from the deepest part of me, must be right.

We are discussing here the disposition behind the deed, the motive behind an actual occurrence. I may never be angry in action, but Jesus Christ demands the complete absence of anger in my attitude. The motive of my motives, the spring of my dreams, must be so right that right deeds will follow naturally.

In Psalm 139, the psalmist realizes that he is too big for himself—and he prays, "O Lord, explore me, search me out, and see if there is any way of grief in me; trace out the dreams of my dreams, the motives of my motives, make these right;

and lead me in the way everlasting." What we call "deliverance from sin" is not a deliverance only from conscious sins; it is deliverance from sin in God's sight, and He can see down into regions I know nothing about. By the marvelous atonement of Jesus Christ, applied to me by the Holy Spirit, God can purify the springs of my unconscious life until the inclination of my mind is blameless in His sight.

Beware of polishing off the radical aspect of our Lord's teaching by saying that God puts something in us to counteract our wrong disposition—that is a compromise. Jesus never teaches us to curb and suppress the wrong disposition; He gives us a totally new disposition. He alters our mainspring of action. Our Lord's teaching can be interpreted only by the new Spirit which He puts in us. It can never be taken as a series of rules and regulations.

A person cannot imitate the disposition of Jesus Christ—either it is there, or it isn't. When the Son of God is formed in me, He is formed in my human nature, and I have to put on "the new man" (Ephesians 4:24) in accordance with His life, obeying Him. Then His disposition will work through me all the time.

We make our character out of our disposition. Character is something we make, disposition is what we are born with; but when we are born again we are given a new disposition. People make their own character, but we cannot make our disposition—that is a gift. Our natural disposition is given to us by heredity, but by regeneration God gives us the disposition of His Son.

Jesus Christ is pure to the very depths of His motives, and if His disposition can be formed in me, then I begin to see how I can be pure also. "Do not marvel that I said to you, 'You must be born again'" (John 3:7). If I let God alter my heredity, I will become devoted to Him, and Jesus Christ will have gained a disciple. Many of us who call ourselves Christians are not really devoted to Jesus Christ.

Our Lord goes behind the law to the disposition. Everything He says is impossible unless He can put His Spirit into me and remake me from within—then I begin to see how it can be done. When we are born from above, we don't need to pretend to be saints; we cannot help being saints. Am I going to be a spiritually real person or a nicely dressed fraud? Am I a pauper in spirit or proud of my own earnestness? We can be so tremendously in earnest that we are blinded by our earnestness—and never see that God is more in earnest than we are. Thank God for the absolute poverty of spirit that receives from Him all the time.

There is only one way in which you as a disciple will know that Jesus has altered your disposition, and that is by trying circumstances. When circumstances put you to the test, rather than feeling resentment you experience a most amazing change inside. You say, "Praise God, this is an amazing alteration! I know now that God has changed me, because if this had happened to me before I would have been sour and irritable and sarcastic and spiteful. But now there is a well of sweetness in me which I know never came from myself." The proof that God has altered our disposition is not that we persuade ourselves that He has. Rather, we prove He has when circumstances put us to the test.

Criticism of Christians is not wrong, it is absolutely right. When we say we are born again, we are put under scrutiny, and rightly so. If we are born again of the Holy Spirit and have the life of Jesus in us by means of His cross, we must show it in the way we walk and talk and transact all our business.

## Temper of Mind and Truth of Manner •
## Matthew 5:23–26

In these verses, our Lord uses another illustration familiar in His day. If a man, taking a Passover lamb to the priest as an offering, remembered he had leaven in his house, he had to go back and remove the leaven before he brought his offering. We do not carry lambs to sacrifice any more, but the spiritual meaning of the illustration is tremendous—it emphasizes the difference between reality and sincerity.

"If, when you come to the altar," Jesus says, essentially, "you remember that your brother has something against you, don't say another word to *me*—go and be reconciled to your brother. Then come and offer your gift." Jesus does not command the other person. He says, *"You* go." He does not say, "Go halfway," but, "First *go."* There is no question of your rights.

Talk about practical truth that hits us where we live! A person cannot stand as a fraud before Jesus Christ for one second. The Holy Spirit makes us sensitive to things we never thought of before. Never object to the Holy Spirit's intense sensitivity in you when He is educating you down to the smallest point; never discard a conviction. If it is important enough for the Spirit to bring it to your mind, that is the thing He wants to address.

The test Jesus gives is not the truth of our manner but the temper of our mind. Many of us are wonderfully truthful in manner, but our temper of mind is rotten in God's sight. The thing Jesus alters is the temper of mind.

When Jesus says, "If you are offering your gift at the altar and there *remember,*" He is not saying, "there you rake up some small thing by a morbid sensitivity." (That is where Satan gets hold of immature Christians and makes them hyper-conscientious.) No, Jesus' teaching is that you "remember that your brother or sister has something against you." The inference is that the Holy Spirit brings this thing to your memory. If that happens, never check it—say "Yes, Lord, I recognize it," and obey Him at once however humiliating it may be.

It is impossible to do this unless God has altered your temper of mind. But if you are indeed a saint, you will find you have no difficulty doing what otherwise would be an impossible humiliation. The attitude that will not allow the Son of God to rule is the attitude of my claim to my right to myself. This, not immorality, is the essence of sin: "I will exercise my right to myself in this particular matter." But if my disposition has been altered, I will obey Jesus at all costs.

Watch the thing that makes you snort morally. If you have not had the temper of your mind altered by Jesus Christ, then when the Holy Spirit reminds you of something to make right, you will say, "No, really. I am not going to make that up when I was in the right and they were in the wrong." Unless you are willing to yield your right to yourself on that point absolutely, you don't need to pray any more—there is a barrier higher than Calvary between you and God.

That is the temper of mind in all of us until it is altered. When it has been altered, the new temper of mind makes reconciliation as natural as breathing, and to our astonishment we find we now can do what we could not before. The instant you obey, you find the temper of your mind is real. Jesus Christ makes us real, not merely sincere. People who are sincere without being real are not hypocrites; they are perfectly earnest and honest, and want to fulfill what Jesus wants, but they really cannot. That is because they have not received the One who makes them real—the Holy Spirit.

Jesus Christ brings us to the practical test. It is not that I *say* I am pure in heart, but that I *prove* I am by my deeds—I am sincere not only in manner but in the attitude of my mind. All through the Sermon on the Mount the same truth is brought out. "Unless your righteousness *exceeds* the righteousness of the scribes and Pharisees . . ." We have to fulfill all the old law and much more, and the only way we can do that is by letting Jesus alter us within—and by remembering that everything He tells us to do we *can* do. The whole point of our Lord's teaching is this: "Obey me, and you will find you have a wealth of power within."

### Lust and License • Matthew 5:27–28

Without apology, our Lord goes to the root of the matter every time. Is discussing lust sordid? It is insanely sordid, but sin is insanely sordid—and there is no excuse in false modesty or refusing to face the music of the Devil's work in this life. Jesus Christ faced it, and He makes us face it too.

Our natural idea of purity is that it means obedience to certain laws and regulations. But that is actually prudery, and there is nothing prudish in the Bible. The Bible insists on purity, not prudery. There are bald, shocking statements in the Bible, but from cover to cover the Bible will do nothing to harm the pure in heart; it is to the impure in heart that these things are corrupting.

If Jesus Christ can only make us prudish, we would be horrified to go and work among the moral abominations of the unsaved world. But with the purity Jesus Christ puts inside us, He can take us where He went himself, making us capable of facing the vilest moral corruption without being stained. He will keep us as pure as He is himself.

We as Christians are often scandalized at public immoralities because our sense of social honor is upset. But are we cut to the heart when we see a person living in pride against God? When the Holy Spirit is at work He gives us new standards of judgment and proportion.

Remember that there is a secret immorality in every religious sentiment not carried out on its right level. That is the way human nature is constituted: whenever you permit an emotion but do not carry it out on its legitimate level, it will react on an illegitimate level. You have no business harboring an emotion which you can see will be wrong in the end. Hold it at the door of your mind as in a vice, and allow it to go no further.

God does not give a person a new body when he or she is saved: the body is the same, but a new disposition is given. God alters the mainspring—He puts love in the place of lust. What is lust? The impatience of desire, the feeling that says, "I must have it at once." Love can wait seven years; lust cannot wait two seconds. Esau and his bowl of stew is a picture of lust (see Genesis 25:29–34); Jacob serving for Rachel is a picture of love (see Genesis 29:15–20). In these verses, lust is put on the lowest level—but remember that lust runs from the lowest depths of immorality right up to the very height of spiritual life. Jesus Christ penetrates straight down to the basis of our desires.

If anyone is ever going to stand where lust can't reach, it can only be because Jesus has altered his or her disposition. It would be impossible to avoid lust unless Jesus Christ can do what He says He can. A disciple has to be free from the degradation of lust, and the marvel of redemption is that Jesus can free His disciples from it.

Jesus Christ's claim is that He can do for human beings what we cannot do for ourselves. Jesus does not alter our human nature; it does not need altering. He alters the mainspring. The great marvel of the salvation of Jesus is that He changes heredity. License is rebellion against all law: "I will do what I like and care about no one else." Liberty is the ability to perform the law—when there is no independence of God in my makeup.

Do you see how we are growing? The disciples were being taught by Jesus Christ to expect to be pure. But purity is too deep for us to get to naturally. The only exhibition of purity is the purity in the heart of our Lord, and that is the purity

He implants in us. He says we will know whether we have that purity by the temper of mind we exhibit when we come up against things that before would have awakened in us lust and self-desire. It is not only a question of possibility on the inside, but of a possibility that shows itself in performance. That is the only test there is: "He who practices righteousness is righteous" (1 John 3:7).

### Direction of Discipline • Matthew 5:29–30

If God has altered our disposition, why do we need discipline? And yet in these verses our Lord speaks of very stern discipline—to the point of removing the right hand and the right eye. The reason for this need of discipline is that our bodies have been used by the wrong disposition, and when the new disposition is put inside us, the old physical body is *not* taken away—it is left there for us to discipline and turn into an obedient servant to the new disposition (see Romans 6:19).

> *"If your right hand causes you to sin, cut it off and cast it from you; for it is more profitable for you that one of your members perish, than for your whole body to be cast into hell."*

What does that mean? It means absolute, unflinching sternness in dealing with the good things in yourself that are not the best. In every person, "the good is the enemy of the best"—the good that is not good enough. Your right hand is not a bad thing; it is one of the best things you have. But Jesus says if your right hand interferes with the development of your spiritual life, hindering you in following His precepts, cut it off and throw it away from you.

Jesus Christ spoke rugged truth. He was never ambiguous, and He says it is better to be maimed than damned—better to live your life lame in people's sight and lovely in God's than to be lovely in human eyes and lame in God's. In these verses, Jesus describes a maimed life to begin with; we may look all right in the sight of other people, but we are remarkably twisted and wrong in the sight of God.

One of our Lord's principles that we are slow to grasp is this: the only basis of the spiritual is the sacrifice of the natural. The natural life is neither moral nor immoral; I make it moral or immoral by my ruling disposition. Jesus teaches that the natural life is meant for sacrifice. We can give it as a gift to God, which is the only way to make it spiritual (see Romans 12:1–2).

That is where Adam failed. He refused to sacrifice the natural life and make it spiritual by obeying God's voice. In that he sinned—the sin of claiming a right to himself. Why did God demand that I sacrifice the natural to the spiritual? He did not. God's order was that the natural should be transformed into the spiritual by obedience. It was sin that made it necessary for the natural to be sacrificed, which is a very different thing.

If you are going to be spiritual, you must trade away the natural—sacrifice it. But if you say, "I do not want to sacrifice the natural for the spiritual," then Jesus says you must trade away the spiritual. That is not a punishment but an eternal principle.

This discipline is the harshest imposed on humanity. There is nothing more heroic, more grand than the Christian life. Spirituality is not a sweet tendency toward goodness in people who are afraid to be bad; spirituality is the possession of the life of God, which is masculine in its strength. He will make the most corrupt, twisted, sin-stained life entirely spiritual—if He is obeyed. Purity is strong and fierce, and the person who is going to be pure for Jesus Christ's sake has a glorious, excellent job ahead.

When Jesus Christ has altered our disposition, we have to bring our body into harmony with the new disposition. We must cause our body to exercise the new disposition, and this can only be done by stern discipline—which will mean cutting off a great many things for the sake of our spiritual life.

Some things are like a right hand and eye to us, yet we don't dare use them. The world around us says, "How absurd! Why would you cut that off? What is wrong with a right hand?" They will call us fanatics and cranks. If you have never been a crank or a fanatic, it is a pretty sure sign that you have never begun to take life seriously.

In the beginning, the Holy Spirit will keep us from doing many things that may be perfectly right for everyone else. But they will not be right for us. No one can decide for another person what is to be cut off, and we have no right to use our own Spirit-prompted limitations to criticize others.

Jesus says, to further our spiritual character, we must be prepared to be limited fools in the sight of others. If we are only willing to give up wrong things for Jesus Christ, we should never talk about being in love with Him. If you want to say, "Why shouldn't I? There is no harm in it," go and do it—but remember that the construction of spiritual character is doomed as soon as you take that line.

If he or she knows how, any person will give up the wrong things. But are we prepared to give up the best we have for Jesus Christ? The only right we as Christian have is the right to give up our rights.

## The Account with Practice

*(Matthew 5:31–37)*

By *practice* I mean the continual behavior of each person, that which nobody sees or knows except we ourselves. Habit, then, is the result of practice; by continually doing a thing it becomes second nature.

The difference between people is not a difference of personal power, but that some people are disciplined while others are not. The difference is not the degree of mental power but the degree of mental discipline. If we have taught ourselves how to think, we will have mental power *plus* the discipline of having it under control. Beware of impulsiveness—it is the characteristic of a child, but it ought not to be the characteristic of an adult. Impulsiveness means we have not disciplined ourselves. Uncontrolled impulse is undisciplined power.

Habits are purely mechanical, and whenever we form a habit it makes a material difference in the brain. The material of the brain alters very slowly, but it does alter—and by doing something repeatedly, our brain is changed. It becomes easier to do that thing again and again, until at last we become unconscious of doing it. When we are regenerated, by the power and the presence of God, we can re-form every habit that is not in accordance with His life.

Never form a habit gradually. Do it at once, sharply and definitely, and never allow a break. We have to learn to form habits according to the dictates of the Spirit of God. The power and the practice must go together.

When we fail it is because we have not practiced—we have not brought the mechanical part of our nature into line. If we keep practicing, what we practice becomes our second nature. In a crisis we will find that not only does God's grace stand by us, but our own nature does also. The practicing is our responsibility, not God's, and crises reveal whether or not we have been practicing. We do not fail because of the Devil, but because of carelessness on our part—the fact that we have not disciplined ourselves.

In verses 31 and 32, Jesus discusses marriage which, along with money, forms the basic structure of personal and social life. They are the touchstones of reality, and around these two things the Holy Spirit works all the time.

Marriage is one of the mountain peaks on which God's thunder blasts souls to hell, or on which His light transforms human lives to the eternal heavens. Jesus Christ fearlessly faces the question of sin and wrong, and He teaches us to face it fearlessly also. There is no circumstance so dark and complicated, no life so twisted, that He cannot put right.

The Bible was not written for babes and fools. It was written for men and women who have to face hell's facts in this life—as well as heaven's facts. Some lives present a happy face but have hideous tragedy behind them. If Jesus Christ cannot touch those, what good is His salvation? But, praise

God, He can. He can alter our disposition, and He can alter the dreams of our dreams until lust no longer lives in them.

## Speech and Sincerity • Matthew 5:33

*Sincerity* means that your appearance and your reality are exactly the same. "Remember," Jesus seems to say, "you stand in the courtroom of God, not of men; practice the right kind of speech and your Father in heaven will back up all that is true. If you have to back it up yourself, it is of the evil one."

We should not have to call on anyone to back up our word; our word ought to be sufficient, and whether others believe us or not is a matter of indifference. We all know people whose word is their bond; there is no need for anyone to back up their word, as their character and life are quite sufficient. Hold your speech until you can convey the sincerity of your mind through it. Until the Son of God is formed in us we are not sincere, not even honest—but when His life comes into us, He makes us honest with ourselves and generous and kind toward others.

There is a danger in being able to discuss God's truth easily—because, frequently, that is where it ends. If we can express the truth well, the danger is that we do not go on to know more. Most of us can talk piously; we have the practice but not the power. Jesus is saying that our conversation should spring from the basis of His Spirit in us, so that everyone who listens is built up by it.

Unaffected sincerity always builds up; corrupt communication makes us low and unloving. There are people who never say a bad word, yet their influence is devilish. Don't pay attention to the outside of the dish, pay attention to what is in the dish. Practice the speech that corresponds with the life of the Son of God in you, and slowly and surely your speech and your sincerity will be in accord.

### Irreverent Reverence • Matthew 5:34–36

In our Lord's day, as in ours, there was a common habit of backing up ordinary assertions with an appeal to the name of God. Jesus rejects that. He says never to call on anything in the nature of God to attest what you say. Just speak simply and truthfully, realizing that truth in human beings is the same as truth in God.

To call God as a witness to back up what you say is nearly always a sign that what you are saying is not true. Similarly, if you can find reasons for the truth of what you say, it is proof that what you say is not strictly true—if it were, you would never have to find reasons to prove it. Jesus Christ advocates a truthfulness that never takes knowledge of itself.

Our Lord stands against "irreverent reverence," that is, talking flippantly about things that ought only to be mentioned with the greatest reverence.

### Integrity • Matthew 5:37

*Integrity* means unimpaired purity of heart. God can make our words the exact expression of the disposition He has put in us. Jesus taught by example and by precept that no one should stand up for his or her own honor but only for the honor of another.

Our Lord was never concerned with His own honor; He "made Himself of no reputation" (Philippians 2:7). People called Him a glutton and a drunkard (see Matthew 11:19), a madman and demon-possessed (see Mark 3:21–22)—and He never opened His mouth. But as soon as they said a word against His Father's honor, He not only opened His mouth, but He said some terrible things (see Mark 11:15–18).

Jesus Christ by His Spirit alters our standard of honor, and as disciples we should never care what people say of us. But we will care tremendously what people say about Jesus Christ; we realize that our Lord's honor, not our own, is at stake in our lives. What is the thing that stirs your emotion? That is an indication of where you live.

Scandal should be treated as you treat mud on your clothes. If you try to deal with it while it is wet, you rub the mud into the cloth itself. But if you leave it till the mud is dry, you can flick it off with a touch. It will be gone without a trace. Leave scandal alone; never touch it.

Let people do what they like with your truth, but never try to explain it. Jesus never explained anything. We are always explaining, and we get into tangles by not leaving things alone. We need to pray a prayer like St. Augustine's: "O Lord, deliver me from this lust of always vindicating myself."

In the matter of praise, when we are not sure we've done well, we like to find out what other people think. When we are certain we have done well, we do not care an atom whether people praise us or not. It is the same with regard to fear: we all know people who say they are not afraid, but the very fact that they say it proves they are. We have to learn to live on the line of integrity all through.

Another truth we do not sufficiently realize is the influence of what we think over what we say. A person may say wonderfully truthful things, but that person's thinking is what matters. It is possible to say truthful things in a truthful manner and to tell a lie in our thinking. I can repeat to another person what I heard you say, word for word, with every detail scientifically accurate, and yet convey a lie in saying it—because the temper of my mind is different from the temper of your mind when you said it. A lie is not a lack of precision in speech; a lie is in the motive. I may be actually truthful and an absolute liar. It is not the literal words that count but their influence on others.

Suspicion is always of the Devil, and it is the cause of people saying more than they need say. In that aspect, it "is from the evil one." If we submit children to a skeptical atmosphere, calling into question all they say, it will instill their habit of backing up what they say: "Well, ask him if you don't believe me." Such a thought would never occur to a child naturally; it occurs when the child has to talk to suspicious people who continually say, "Now I don't know whether what you are saying is true." The child gets the idea that truth is not spoken unless someone backs it up. It never occurs to a pure, honest heart to back up what it says. It is a wounding insult to be met with suspicion, and that is why from the first a child ought never to be submitted to suspicion.

## The Account with Persecution
*(Matthew 5:38–42)*

### Insult • Matthew 5:38–39

If a disciple is going to follow Jesus Christ, he or she must prepare not only for purity and practice, but also for persecution. The picture our Lord gives in this passage is not familiar to us. In the East, a slap on the cheek is the greatest form of insult—its equivalent with us would be spitting in the face. Epictetus, the first-century philosopher born a Roman slave, said that a slave would rather be thrashed to death than flicked on the cheek.

But Jesus says, "Whoever slaps you on your right cheek, turn the other to him also." The Sermon on the Mount indicates that when we are on Jesus Christ's errands, we should take no time to stand up for ourselves. Personal insult will be the saint's occasion for revealing the incredible sweetness of the Lord Jesus.

The Sermon on the Mount hits where it is meant to hit, and it hits every time. Jesus basically says, "When someone slaps you on your right cheek, as my representative, pay no attention"—that is, show a disposition equivalent to turning the other cheek too. Either Jesus Christ was insane to say such things, or He was the Son of God.

By nature, if a man does not hit back it is because he is a coward. Supernaturally, it is the outward expression of the Son of God in him. Both have the same appearance; the hypocrite and the saint are alike in the public eye. Saints exhibit a meekness which is contemptible in the eyes of the world; that is the immense humiliation of being a Christian. Our strength has to be the strength of the Son of God, and "He was crucified in weakness" (2 Corinthians 13:4). Do the impossible, and as soon as you do, you know that God alone has made it possible.

These things apply to a disciple of Jesus and to no one else. The only way to interpret the words of God is to let the Holy Spirit interpret them for us. Jesus said that the Holy Spirit would bring back to our remembrance what He has said (see John 14:26), and His counsel is this: when you come across personal insult you must not only not resent it, you must make it an occasion of exhibiting the Son of God.

The secret of discipleship is personal devotion to a personal Lord, and we are open to the same charge as Jesus was—that of inconsistency (though Jesus Christ was never inconsistent to God). There is more than one kind of consistency. There is the consistency of a little child, who is never the same, always changing and developing, consistently; and there is the consistency of a brick wall, a petrified consistency. Christians are to be consistent only to the life of the Son of God in them, not consistent to hard-and-fast creeds.

People pour themselves into creeds, and almighty God has to blast them out of their prejudices before they become devoted to Jesus Christ. What the Scottish preacher Thomas Chalmers called "the expulsive power of a new affection" is what Christianity supplies. The reality of the life of the Son of God in us must show itself in the appearance of our lives.

The miracle of regeneration is necessary before we can live the Sermon on the Mount. Only the Son of God can live it, and if God can form in us the life of His Son as introduced in human history, we begin to see how we can live it too. That is Jesus Christ's message: "Do not marvel that I said to you, 'You must be born again'" (John 3:7; see also Luke 1:35).

### Extortion • Matthew 5:40

This passage describes another picture unfamiliar to us, but one that had tremendous meaning in our Lord's day. If a man's cloak and coat were taken from him as the result of a lawsuit, he could borrow back the coat to sleep in at night. Jesus uses the illustration to point out what we are going to meet with as His disciples, saying in essence, "If they extort anything from you while you are in my service, let them have it and go on with your work. If you are my disciple, you will have no time to stand up for yourself."

Never insist on your rights. The Sermon on the Mount does not say, "Do your duty." It says, "Do what is *not* your duty." It is never your duty "not to resist an evil person" (Matthew 5:39)—that is only possible to the Son of God in you.

### Tyranny • Matthew 5:41–42

Under the Roman dominance of the Jewish land, soldiers could compel anyone to carry baggage for a mile. Simon the

Cyrenian is a case in point—Roman soldiers compelled him to be a baggage-carrier for Jesus Christ (Mark 15:21). In this passage, Jesus says, in effect, "If you are my disciple, you will always go the second mile. You will always do more than your duty."

There will be none of this spirit: "Oh well, I can't do any more; they have always misunderstood and misrepresented me." You will go the second mile—not for their sakes, but for Jesus Christ's. We would have had a sorry prospect if God had not gone the second mile with us.

The first thing God requires of a person is to be born from above; then, when the Christian goes the second mile for other people, it is the Son of God inside who does it. The only right we as Christians have is the right not to insist upon our rights. Every time I insist upon my rights I hurt the Son of God (see Hebrews 6:6). I can prevent the Son of God being hurt if I take the blows myself, but if I refuse to take them, they will go back on Him (see Colossians 1:24).

Verse 42 is an arena for theological acrobats: "Give to him who asks you, and from him who wants to borrow from you do not turn away." That is the statement either of a madman or of God incarnate. We always say we do not know what Jesus Christ means when we know perfectly well He means something that is a blunt impossibility unless He can remake us and make it possible. With terrific force, Jesus brings us straight up against the impossible—and until we get to the place of despair we will never receive from Him the grace that enables us to do the impossible and to manifest His Spirit.

These statements of Jesus revolutionize all our conceptions of charity. Much of our modern philanthropy is based on the motive of giving to the poor because "they deserve it," or because we are distressed at seeing poor people. Jesus never taught charity from those motives. His rule was, "Give to the one who asks you, not because he deserves it, but because I tell you to." The great motive in all giving is Jesus Christ's command.

We can find a hundred and one reasons for not obeying our Lord's commands, because we will trust our own reasoning rather than His—and our reason does not take God into the calculation. How do we argue? By asking things like, "Does this man deserve what I am giving him?" As soon as you talk like that, the Spirit of God says, "Who are you? Do *you* deserve more than other people the blessings you have?"

"Give to him who asks you." Why do we always make this about money? The blood of most of us seems to run in gold. Our Lord makes no mention of money. The reason we make it about money is because that is where our heart is. Peter said, "Silver and gold I do not have, but what I do have I give you" (Acts 3:6). God grant that we may understand that the spring of giving is not impulse nor inclination, but the inspiration of the Holy Spirit. I give because Jesus tells me to.

The way Christians wriggle and twist and compromise over this verse springs from unfaithfulness to the ruling providence of our heavenly Father. We enthrone common sense as God and say, "It's crazy. If I give to everyone who asks, every beggar in town will be at my door." Just try it. I have yet to find the person who obeyed Jesus Christ's command who did not realize that God restrains those who beg.

If we try to apply Jesus Christ's principles literally, without the indwelling Spirit, there will be no proof that God is with us. But when we are rightly related to God and are letting the Holy Spirit apply these words to our circumstances, we will find the protective hand of God. If ever God's ruling is seen, it is seen when a disciple obeys Jesus Christ's commands.

# Chapter Three

# Incarnate Wisdom and Individual Reason

*Matthew 5:43–6:34*

We live in two universes: the universe of common sense, in which we come into contact with things by sight, sound, smell, taste, and touch; and the universe of revelation, with which we come in contact by faith. The wisdom of God fits the two universes exactly—the one interprets the other.

Jesus Christ is the expression of the wisdom of God. If we take the commonsense universe and discard the revelation of Jesus Christ, we make what He says foolishness, because He talks from the universe of revelation all the time. Jesus Christ lived in the revelation world that we do not see—and until we get into His world we do not understand His teaching at all. In Him we find that the universe of revelation and the universe of common sense were made one; if they are ever to be one in us it can only be by receiving the heredity of Jesus—the Holy Spirit.

In the commonsense universe we need intellectual curiosity, but when we enter the domain from which Jesus Christ talks, intellectual curiosity is ruled out. Moral obedience is the absolute requirement. "If anyone wills to do His will, he shall know . . ." (John 7:17).

If we are going to find out the secrets of the world we live in, we must work at it. God does not encourage laziness. He has given us instruments by which we can explore this universe and we do it entirely by intellectual curiosity; but when we come to the domain that Jesus Christ reveals, no amount of studying or curiosity will avail a tiny bit. Our ordinary commonsense faculties are of no use; we cannot see or taste God; we can argue with Him, but we cannot get at Him by our senses at all. Common sense is likely to say there is nothing other than this physical universe.

So how are we to get into contact with this other universe to which Jesus Christ belongs and from which He speaks? We touch the revelation facts of God's universe by the faith worked in us by the Spirit of God; then, as we develop in understanding, the two universes are slowly made one in us. They never agree outside Jesus Christ.

An understanding of redemption is not necessary to salvation any more than an understanding of life is necessary before we can be born into it. Jesus Christ did not come to found religion, nor did He come to found civilization—they were both here before He came. Jesus came to make us spiritually real in every domain. In Jesus Christ there was nothing secular and sacred, it was all simply real—and He makes His disciples like himself.

# Divine Rule of Life

*(Matthew 5:43–48)*

In these verses our Lord lays down a divine rule which we—by His Spirit—have to apply to every circumstance and condition of our lives. Our Lord does not make statements that we have to follow literally; if He did we would not grow in grace. In the realm of God it is a *spiritual* following, and we have to rely upon His Spirit to teach us to apply His statements to the various circumstances of our lives.

### Exhortation • Matthew 5:43–44

Our Lord's exhortation here is to be generous in our behavior to all people, whether they are good or bad. The marvel of the divine love is that God exhibits His love not only to good people but to bad people.

In our Lord's parable of the two sons (Luke 15:11–32), we can understand the father loving the prodigal son, but he also exhibits his love to the elder brother, for whom we feel a strong dislike. Beware of walking in the spiritual life according to your natural affinities. We all have natural attractions—some people we like and others we do not; some people we get along with well, and others we do not. Never let those likes and dislikes be the rule of your Christian life. "If we walk in the light as He is in the light, we have fellowship with one another" (1 John 1:7). That means God gives us fellowship with people for whom we have no natural affinity.

### Example • Matthew 5:45

Woven into our Lord's divine rule of life is His reference to our example. Our example is not a good man, not even a good Christian man, but *God himself.* We do not allow the big surprise of this to take hold of our minds.

Nowhere does Jesus say, "Follow the best example you have, follow Christians, watch those who love me and follow them." He says, "Follow your Father in heaven." Why? That you may be good people? That you may be lovable to all people? No, "that you may be sons of your Father in heaven"— and that implies a strong family likeness to Jesus Christ. The example of a disciple is almighty God and no one less; not the best person you know, nor the finest saint you have ever read about, but God himself.

*"That you may be sons of your Father in heaven."*

Our Lord's exhortation to us is to love our fellow human beings as God has loved us. The love of God is not like the love of a father or a mother; it is the love *of God*. "God demonstrates *His own love* toward us" (Romans 5:8). God's love is revealed in that He laid down His life for His enemies, and Jesus tells us to love our fellow humans as God has loved us. As disciples of Jesus, we are to identify ourselves with God's interests in other people, to show them what God has shown us. God will give us ample opportunity in our actual lives to prove that we are perfect as our Father in heaven is perfect.

"You have heard that it was said, 'You shall love your neighbor and hate your enemy.' But I say to you, love your enemies" (Matthew 5:43–44). Again, I want to emphasize the fact that the teaching of Jesus Christ does not appear at first to be what it truly is. At first it appears to be beautiful and pious and lukewarm—but before long it becomes a ripping and tearing torpedo that splits to atoms every preconceived notion a person ever had.

It takes a long time to get the full force of our Lord's statements. "I say unto you, love your enemies." That is an easy thing when you have no enemies; an impossible thing when you do. "Bless those who curse you." It's easy when no one is cursing you, but impossible when someone is. "Do good to those who hate you, and pray for those who spitefully use you." It seems easy to do all this when we have no enemies, when no one is cursing or persecuting us. But if we have an enemy who slanders and annoys and systematically harasses us, and we read Jesus Christ's statement "I say to you, *love your enemies*"—how are we going to do it?

Unless Jesus Christ can remake us within, His teaching is the biggest mockery human ears ever heard. Talk about the Sermon on the Mount being an ideal! It tears people with despair—the very thing Jesus means it to do, for when once we realize that we cannot love our enemies, we cannot bless those who curse us, we cannot come anywhere near the standard revealed in the Sermon on the Mount, *then* we are in a condition to receive from God the disposition that will enable us to love our enemies, to pray for those who spitefully use us, to do good to those who hate us.

"I say to you, love your enemies." Jesus does not say, "Love everyone." The Bible never speaks vaguely, it always speaks definitely. People talk about loving "humanity" and loving "the lost." Jesus says, "Love your enemies." Our Lord does not say, "*Bless* your enemies," He says, "*Love* your enemies." He does not say, "*Love* those who curse you," He says, "*Bless* those who curse you." "*Do good* to those who hate you"—not *bless* them. He does not say, "*Do good* to those who spitefully use you," He says, "*Pray* for those who spitefully use you."

Each one of these commands is stamped with sheer impossibility to the natural person. If we reverse the order Jesus has given it could be done with strain, but kept in His order I defy any person on earth to be able to do it unless he or she has been regenerated by God the Holy Spirit. When people do love their enemies, we know that God has done a tremendous work in them—and everyone else knows it too.

## Expression • Matthew 5:46–48

Christian character is not expressed by good-doing, but by God-likeness. It is not sufficient to do good, to do the right thing—we must have our goodness stamped by the image and inscription of God. It is supernatural all through.

The secret of a Christian's life is that the supernatural is made natural by the grace of God. The way that is expressed is not in our times of communion with God, but in the practical details of life. The proof that we have been regenerated is that when we come in contact with the things that upset us, we find to our astonishment that we have a power to keep wonderfully poised in the center of it all. It is a power we did not have before, a power that is only explained by the cross of Jesus Christ.

Verse 48 is a re-emphasis of verse 20. The perfection of verse 48 refers to the disposition of God in me—"you shall be perfect, just as your Father in heaven is perfect"—and not just in a future state. What Jesus is saying is this: "You shall be perfect as your Father in heaven is perfect if you let me work that perfection in you."

If the Holy Spirit has transformed us within, we will not exhibit good human characteristics, but divine characteristics in our human nature. There is only one type of holiness and that is the holiness of God—and Jesus gives almighty God as our example. How many of us have measured ourselves by that standard, the standard of a purity of heart in which God can see nothing to blame?

May this divine rule of our Lord's bring us to the court of the standard of Jesus Christ. His claim is measured by these tremendous statements of His. He can take the vilest piece of "broken earthenware," He can take you and me and fit us exactly to the expression of the divine life in us. It is not a question of putting the statements of our Lord in front of us and trying to live up to them, but of receiving His Spirit and finding that we *can* live up to them as He brings them to our remembrance and applies them to our circumstances.

God grant that we may have the courageous range of faith that is required. "You shall be perfect, just as your Father in heaven is perfect"—and people will see that I am a good man? Never! If it is ever recorded of me, "What a good man that is," I have been a betrayer somewhere. If we fix our eyes on our own goodness we will soon rot in our spiritual life. All our righteousness is "like filthy rags" (Isaiah 64:6) unless it is the blazing holiness of Jesus in us uniting us with Him, until we see nothing but Jesus first, Jesus second, and Jesus third. Then when people take knowledge of us, they will not say that we are good, that we have a wonderful cleanness, but that Jesus Christ has done something wonderful in us. Always focus on the source of spiritual blessings—Jesus Christ himself.

Our Lord says, in verse 30, "it is more profitable for you that one of your members perish, than for your whole body to be cast into hell." Here He is referring to a *maimed* life. In verse 48 He says, "you shall be perfect, just as your Father in heaven is perfect." Is our Father in heaven maimed? Does He have a right arm cut off, a right eye plucked out? No, in verse 48 Jesus completes the picture He began to give in verse 30.

Our Lord's statements embrace the whole of the spiritual life from the beginning to the end. In verses 29–30, He pictures a maimed life: in verse 48 He pictures a complete life of holiness. Holiness means a perfect balance between my disposition and the laws of God. The maimed life is the characteristic at the beginning, and if we have not had that characteristic it is questionable whether we have ever received the Holy Spirit.

What the world calls fanaticism is the entrance into life. We have to begin our lives with God as maimed souls; the swing of the pendulum makes us go to the opposite extreme of what we were in the life of the world. We are so afraid of being fanatical; would to God we were as afraid of being dull and flat. We should a thousand times rather be fanatical in the beginning than dull creatures all our lives, limp and useless. May we get to the place where we are willing to cut off the right arm, to pluck out the right eye, to enter into the spiritual life maimed, having cut off whatever we needed to, however beautiful. And blessed be the name of God, we shall find that He will bring every life that obeys Him to a complete unity.

Always make allowances for people when they first enter into the spiritual life—they have to enter on the fanatical line. The danger is if they stay too long in the stage of fanaticism. When fanaticism steps over the bounds, it becomes spiritual lunacy. In the beginning of the life in grace, we have to limit ourselves all round, in right things as well as wrong; but if, when God begins to bring us out of the light of our convictions and into the light of the Lord, we prefer to remain true to our convictions, we become spiritual lunatics. Walking in the light of convictions is a necessary stage, but there is a grander, purer, sterner light to walk in—the light of the Lord.

How impatient we are! When we see a life born from above of the Spirit and the necessary limitations and severances and maimings taking place, we will try to do God's work for Him. Then God has to rap us sharply over the knuckles and say, "Leave that soul in *my* care." Always allow for the swing of the pendulum in yourself and in others. A pendulum does not swing evenly at first; it begins with a tremendous swing to one extreme and only gets back to the right balance gradually. That is how the Holy Spirit brings the grace of God to bear upon our lives. "I do not set aside the grace of God," says Paul (Galatians 2:21).

# Divine Region of Religion
*(Matthew 6:1–18)*

In Matthew 5, our Lord demands that our dispositions be right with Him in our ordinary natural life lived toward people; in Matthew 6, He deals with the domain of our life lived toward God before people. The main idea in the region of religion is this: *Your eyes on God, not on people.*

## Philanthropy • Matthew 6:1–4

It was ingrained, as it were, into the very blood of the Jews, to look after strangers (see Deuteronomy 15:7–8; Leviticus 19:9–10). In our Lord's day, the Pharisees made a tremendous show of giving, but they gave from a play-acting motive that they might "have glory from men." In the women's court of the temple, they would put their money in the boxes with a great clang that sounded like a trumpet. Jesus tells us not to give that way, with the motive to be seen by people, to be known as a generous givers—because, "I say to you, they have their reward." That is all there is to it.

Briefly summed up, these verses mean this: Have no other motive in giving than to please God. In modern philanthropy we are egged on with other motives—"It will do them good." "They need the help." "They deserve it." Jesus Christ never brings out those aspects in His teaching; He allows no other motive in giving than to please God.

In Matthew 5, Jesus says, basically, "Give because I tell you to." Here, He teaches us not to have mixed motives. It is very penetrating to ask ourselves this question: "What was my motive in doing that kind act?" We will be astounded to find how rarely the Holy Spirit gets a chance to fix our motives on being right with God; we mix our motives with a hundred and one other considerations. Jesus Christ makes it steadily simple—one motive only, your eyes on God. "If you are My disciple," He says in essence, "you will never give with any other motive than to please God." The characteristic of Jesus in a disciple is much deeper than doing good things—it is goodness in motive because the disciple has been made loved by the supernatural grace of God.

"But when you do a charitable deed, do not let your left hand know what your right hand is doing"—that is, do good until it is an unconscious habit of life and you do not even know you are doing it. At that point, you will be confused when Jesus Christ detects it. "'Lord, when did we see You hungry and feed You?' . . . Inasmuch as you did it to one of the least of these My brethren, you did it to Me" (Matthew 25:37, 40). That is our Lord's magnanimous interpretation of kind acts that people have never allowed themselves even to think about.

Develop the habit of having such a relationship to God that you do good without knowing it. Then you will no longer trust your own impulse or judgment—you will trust only the inspiration of the Spirit of God. The mainspring of your motives will be the Father's heart, not your own; the Father's understanding, not yours. When you are rightly related to God, He will use you as a channel through which His disposition will flow.

## Prayer • Matthew 6:5–15

Prayer, Jesus says, is to be looked at in the same way as philanthropy—with your eyes on God, not on people. Watch your motive before God; have no other motive in prayer than to know Him. Jesus' statements about prayer, which are so familiar to us, are revolutionary. Stop a moment and ask yourself, "Why do I pray? What is my motive? Is it because I have a personal secret relationship to God known to no one but myself?"

The Pharisees were obliged to pray so many times a day, and they made sure they happened to be in the middle of the city when the prayer hour came—then, in an ostentatious manner, they would give themselves to prayer. Basically, Jesus says, "You should not be like the hypocrites; their motive is to be known as praying people, and, truly, they have their reward."

Our Lord did not say it was wrong to pray on the street corners, but He did say that the motive to "be seen by men" was wrong. "But you, when you pray, go into your room, and when you have shut your door, pray to your Father who is in the secret place"—that is, get a place for prayer where no one imagines that that is what you are doing. Shut the door and talk to God in secret. It is impossible to live the life of a disciple without definite times of secret prayer.

You will find that the place to "go into" is in your business, as you walk along the streets, in the ordinary ways of life when no one dreams you are praying. Then the reward comes openly—a revival here, a blessing there. The Scots have a proverb, "Aye keep a bittie to yersel," and as you go on with God you learn more and more to maintain this secret relationship with God in prayer.

When we pray we give God a chance to work in the unconscious realm of the lives of those for whom we pray. When we come into the secret place it is the Holy Spirit's passion for souls that is at work, not our own passion, and He can work through us as He likes. Religious groups may produce a passion for souls; the Holy Spirit produces a passion for Christ. The great, dominating passion all through the New Testament is for our Lord Jesus Christ.

Jesus also taught the disciples the prayer of patience. If you are right with God and God delays the obvious answer to your prayer, don't misjudge Him, don't think of Him as an unkind friend or an unnatural father or an unjust judge. Keep at it—your prayer will certainly be answered, "for everyone who asks receives" (Matthew 7:8). "Men always ought to pray and not lose heart" (Luke 18:1)—that is, not cave in. "Your heavenly Father will explain it all one day," Jesus seems to say. "He cannot just now because He is developing your character."

In verse 8 Jesus goes to the root of all prayer: "Your Father knows the things you have need of before you ask Him." Common sense says, "Then why ask Him?" But prayer is not just getting things from God; that is a most initial stage. Prayer is getting into perfect communion with God—I tell

Him what I know He knows so that I may get to know it as He does. Jesus essentially says, "Pray because you have a Father, not because it calms you, and give Him time to answer." If the life of Jesus is formed in me by regeneration and I am drawing my breath in the fear of the Lord, the Son of God will press ahead of my common sense and change my attitude to things.

Most of us make the blunder of depending upon our own earnestness, not on God at all. It is confidence in Jesus that tells (see 1 John 5:14). All our fuss and earnestness, all our gifts of prayer, are of no use to Jesus Christ. He pays no attention to them. If you have a gift of prayer, may God wither it up until you learn how to get your prayers inspired by God the Holy Spirit. Do we rely on God or on our own earnestness when we pray? God is never impressed by our earnestness; we are not heard because we are in earnest, but only on the ground of redemption. "Having boldness to enter the Holiest *by the blood of Jesus*" (Hebrews 10:19), and by no other way.

"Your Father knows the things you have need of." Jesus basically tells us, "Remember—your Father is keenly and divinely interested in you, and prayer becomes the chatter of a child to his father." We are inclined to take everything and everyone seriously except God; our Lord took nothing and no one seriously but His Father, and He teaches us to be as children before other people, but in earnest before our Father in heaven. Notice the essential simplicity of our Lord's teaching all through—right towards God, right towards God.

## Penance • Matthew 6:16–18

Penance means putting ourselves into a straitjacket for the sake of disciplining our spiritual character. Physical laziness will upset our spiritual devotion quicker than anything else. If the Devil cannot get at us by enticing to sin, he will get at us by a spiritual sleeping sickness: "Now, you cannot possibly get up in the morning to pray. You are working hard all day and you cannot give that time to prayer. God does not expect it of you." Jesus says God *does* expect it of us.

Penance means doing a hardship to the body for the sake of developing the spiritual life. Put your life through discipline, but don't say a word about it—"do not appear to men to be fasting." The seventeenth-century cleric Jeremy Taylor said that people hang out the sign of the Devil to prove there is an angel within—that is, they wear sad faces and look tremendously severe in order to prove they are holy. In this matter, Jesus taught His disciples to be hypocrites: "But you, when you fast, anoint your head and wash your face"—that is, never allow anyone to imagine you are putting yourself through discipline.

If we ever tell others the discipline we put ourselves through to further our life with God, from that moment the discipline becomes useless. Our Lord counsels us to have a relationship between ourselves and God that our dearest friends on earth could never guess. When you fast, fast to your Father in secret—not before people.

Do not make a cheap martyr of yourself, and never ask for pity. If you are going through a time of discipline, pretend you are not—"do not appear to men to be fasting." The Holy Spirit will apply this to each one of us. There are lines of discipline, lines of limitation—physical and mental and spiritual—and the Holy Spirit will say, "You must not allow yourself this and that." External fasts, intended for display, are of no use—it is the internal fasting that counts.

Fasting from food may be difficult for some, but that is child's play compared with fasting for the development of God's purpose in your life. Fasting means concentration. Five minutes' attention to what Jesus says and solid concentration on it would bring about transactions with God that would end in sanctification.

> *"Do not be like the hypocrites, with a sad countenance. For they disfigure their faces that they may appear to men to be fasting."*

May God destroy forever, as Tennyson described it, "the grief that saps the mind," as well as our luxury of misery and morbid introspection that we indulge in order to develop holiness. Instead, may we bear the shining faces that belong to the sons of God: "They looked to Him and were radiant" (Psalm 34:5).

# Divine Reasonings of Mind
*(Matthew 6:19–24)*

It is a fruitful study to find out what the New Testament says about the mind. The Spirit of God comes through the different writers with the one steady insistence to stir up our minds (see, for example, Philippians 2:5; 2 Peter 1:12–13). Satan comes as an "angel of light" only to those Christians whose hearts are right but whose minds are not stirred up. In these verses in Matthew 6, our Lord deals with the mind and tells us how we are to think and to reason about things. Unless we learn to think in obedience to the Holy Spirit's teaching, we will drift in our spiritual experience without any thinking at all. The confusion arises when we try to think and to reason things out without the Spirit of God.

## Doctrine of Deposit • Matthew 6:19–21

The Holy Spirit teaches us to fasten our thinking upon God. Then when we come to deal with property and money and everything to do with the matters of earth, He reminds us that our real treasure is in heaven. Every effort to persuade myself that my treasure is in heaven is a sure sign that it is not. When my motive has been put right, it will put my thinking right.

"But lay up for yourselves treasures in heaven"—that is, have your banking account in heaven, not on earth. Lay up your confidence in God, not in your common sense. It is the *trial* of your faith that makes you wealthy (see 1 Peter 1:7), and it works in this way: every time you venture out on the life of faith, you will come across something in your actual life that seems to absolutely contradict what your faith in God says you should believe. Go through the trial of faith and lay up your confidence in God, not in your common sense—you will gain wealth in your heavenly banking account and the more you go through the trial of faith the wealthier you will become in the heavenly regions. Ultimately, you will smile through the difficulties and people will wonder where your wealth of trust comes from.

It is a trial of faith all through. The conflict for the Christian is not a conflict with sin, but a conflict over the natural life being turned into the spiritual life. The natural life is not sinful—the disposition that rules the natural life is sinful. When God alters that disposition, we have to turn the natural life into the spiritual by a steady process of obedience to God, and it takes spiritual concentration on God to do it. If you are going to succeed in anything in this world, you must concentrate on it, practice it—and the same is true spiritually.

If you are going to be concentrated on God, there are many things you will find you cannot do—things that may be perfectly legitimate and right for others, but not for you if you are going to concentrate on God. Never let the narrowness of your conscience condemn another person. Maintain the personal relationship, and see that you yourself are concentrated on God—not on your convictions or your point of view, but on God. Whenever you are in doubt about something, push it to its logical conclusion: "Is this the kind of thing that Jesus Christ is after, or the kind of thing Satan is after?" As soon as your decision is made, act on it.

## Doctrine of Division • Matthew 6:22–23

In verse 22, our Lord is using the eye as the symbol of conscience in a person who has been put right by the Holy Spirit. A single eye is essential to correct understanding. One idea runs all through our Lord's teaching—right with God, first, second, and third. If we are born again of the Holy Spirit, we do not persuade ourselves that we are right with God—we *are* right with Him because we have been put right by the Holy Spirit. Then if we walk in the light as God is in the light, that will keep the eye single, and slowly and surely all our actions begin to be put into the right relationship. Everything becomes full of harmony and simplicity and peace.

No one has a single motive unless he or she has been born from above; we have single ambitions, but not single motives. Jesus Christ is the only one with a single motive, and when His Spirit comes into us, the first thing He does is to make us people with a single motive, a single eye to the glory of God. The one motive of Jesus is to turn people into children of God, and the one motive of a disciple is to glorify Jesus Christ.

> *"If therefore the light that is in you is darkness, how great is that darkness!"*

Darkness is my point of view, my right to myself; light is God's point of view. Jesus Christ made the line of demarcation between light and darkness very definite. The danger is that this division becomes blurred. "Men loved darkness rather than light, because their deeds were evil," said Jesus (John 3:19).

## Doctrine of Detachment • Matthew 6:24

> *"You cannot serve God and mammon."*

A man or woman of the world says we can: with a little subtlety and wisdom and compromise (it is called "diplomacy" or "tact"), we can serve both God and mammon. The Devil's temptation to our Lord to fall down and worship him (that is, to compromise) is repeated over and over again in Christian experience. We have to realize that there is a division as high as heaven and as deep as hell between the Christian and the world. "Whoever therefore wants to be a friend of the world makes himself an enemy of God" (James 4:4).

This doctrine of detachment is a fundamental theme of our Lord's and runs all through His teaching. You cannot be good and bad at the same time; you cannot serve God and pursue your own benefit from the service; you cannot make "honesty is the best policy" a motive, because as soon as you do, you cease to be honest.

The questioning the Spirit of God puts people through is the sternest on earth: "Why are you a student for the ministry, a missionary, a preacher of the Gospel?" There should be one consideration only—to stand right with God. When we see that that relationship is the one thing that is never dimmed, all other things will right themselves. But as soon as we lose sight of that relationship, a multitude of motives begin to work and you soon become worn out.

Never compromise with the spirit of mammon. When you are right with God, you become contemptible in the eyes of the world. Put into practice any of the Sermon on the Mount's teaching, and you will be treated with amusement at first; then, if you persist, the world will get annoyed and will detest you.

What will happen, for instance, if you carry out Jesus Christ's teaching in business? Not quite so much success as you bargained for. This is not the age of the glorification of the saints, but the age of their humiliation. Are you prepared to follow Jesus Christ outside the camp, the special camp to which you belong?

"You cannot serve God and mammon." What is mammon? The system of civilized life which organizes itself without considering God. We have to stand absolutely true to God's methods. Thank God for everyone who has learned that the dearest friend on earth is a mere shadow compared with Jesus Christ. There must be a dominant, personal, passionate devotion to Him, and only then are all other relationships right (see Luke 14:26).

Jesus Christ is not teaching ordinary integrity but supernormal integrity, a likeness to our Father in heaven. In the beginning of our spiritual life we must make allowance for the swing of the pendulum. It is not by accident but by the set purpose of God that in the reaction we go to the opposite extreme of all we were before. God breaks us from the old life violently, not gradually—and only when we are right with Him does He bring us back into the domain of people; we are to be *in* the world, but not of it. When we become mature in godliness, God trusts His own honor to us by placing us where the world, the flesh, and the Devil may try us, knowing that "He who is in you is greater than he who is in the world" (1 John 4:4).

## Divine Reasonings of Faith

*(Matthew 6:25–34)*

Faith is our personal confidence in a being whose character we know, but whose ways we cannot trace by common sense. By the "reasonings of faith" I mean the practical outworking in our life of implicit, determined confidence in God. Common sense is mathematical; faith is not—it works on illogical lines. Jesus Christ places the strongest emphasis on faith, and especially on the faith that has been tried.

To have faith tests people for all they are worth. They have to stand in the commonsense universe, in the midst of things which conflict with their faith, and place their confidence in the God whose character is revealed in Jesus Christ. Jesus Christ's statements reveal that God is a being of love and justice and truth; the actual happenings of our immediate circumstances seem to prove He is not. Are we going to remain true to the revelation that God is good? Are we going to be true to His honor, whatever may happen in the actual domain? If we are, we will find that God in His providence makes the two universes—the universe of revelation and the universe of common sense—work together in perfect harmony. Most of us are irreligious in a crisis; we think and act like unbelievers. Only one out of a hundred is daring enough to bank their faith in the character of God.

For understanding in spiritual matters, the golden rule is not intellect but obedience. Discernment in the spiritual world is never gained by intellect; it is in the commonsense world. If a person wants scientific knowledge, intellectual curiosity is the guide; but if that person wants insight into what Jesus Christ teaches, it can only come by obedience.

If things are dark to us spiritually, it is because there is something we will not do. Intellectual darkness comes because of ignorance; spiritual darkness comes because of something I do not intend to obey.

## Careful Carelessness • Matthew 6:25

Jesus does not say, "Blessed is the one who does not think about *anything*." That person is a fool. Jesus says, basically, "Be carefully careless about everything except one thing—your relationship to God." That means to be studiously careful to be careless about how we stand to self-interest, to food, to clothes—for one reason only, that we are set on minding our relationship to God.

Many people are careless about what they eat and drink, and they suffer for it. Some are careless about what they put on, and they look as they have no right to look. Still others are careless over property, and God holds them responsible for it. Jesus is saying that the great care of the life is to put the relationship to God first and everything else second. Our Lord teaches a complete reversal of all our practical sensible reasoning.

Do not make the ruling factor of your life what you will eat or what you will drink; make a zealous concentration on God the one point of your life. The one dominating abandon of our lives should be concentration on God, so every other carelessness is careless in comparison. In Luke 14:26, our Lord lays down the conditions of discipleship, saying that the first condition is personal, passionate devotion to himself until every other devotion is hatred in comparison.

"Do not worry about your life." As soon as we look at these words of our Lord, we find them the most revolutionary of statements. We argue in exactly the opposite way, even the most spiritual of us: "I *must* live, I *must* make so much money, I *must* be clothed and fed." That is how it begins—the great concern of the life is not God, but how we are going to equip ourselves to live.

But Jesus Christ says, "Reverse the order—get rightly related to me first, see that you maintain that as the great care of your life, and never put the concentration of your care on the other things." It is a severe discipline to allow the Holy Spirit to bring us into harmony with the teaching of Jesus in these verses.

## Careful Unreasonableness • Matthew 6:26–29

Jesus declares it unreasonable for a disciple to be careful of all that the natural person says we must be careful over. "Look at the birds of the air, for they neither sow nor reap nor gather into barns; yet your heavenly Father feeds them. Are you not of more value than they? . . . Consider the lilies of the field, how they grow: they neither toil nor spin; and yet I say to you that even Solomon in all his glory was not arrayed like one of these."

Jesus does not use the illustration of the birds and the flowers by accident. He uses it purposely, to show from His standpoint the utter unreasonableness of being so anxious about the means of living. Imagine the sparrows and blackbirds and thrushes worrying about their feathers! Jesus says they do not trouble about themselves at all—the thing that makes them what they are is not their thought for themselves, but the thought of the Father in heaven.

A bird is a hardworking little creature, but it does not work for its feathers—it obeys the law of its life and becomes what it is. Jesus Christ's argument is that if we concentrate on the life He gives us, we will be perfectly free for all other things because our Father is watching the inner life. We have to maintain obedience to the Holy Spirit, who is the real principle of our life, and then God will supply the "feathers." Aren't we "of more value than they"?

It is useless to mistake a careful consideration of circumstances for that which produces character. We cannot produce an inner life by always watching the outer. Jesus says, as a disciple, consider your hidden life with God; pay attention to the Source and God will look after the outflow.

The lily obeys the law of its life in the surroundings in which it is placed. Imagine a lily hauling itself out of its pot and saying, "I don't think I look exactly right here." The lily's duty is to obey the law of its life where it is put by the gardener. "Watch your life with God," Jesus says. "See that it is right and you will grow as the lily."

We are all inclined to say, "I would be all right if only I were somewhere else." There is only one way to develop spiritually, and that is by concentrating on God. Don't bother about whether you are growing in grace or whether you are being of use to others. Just believe on Jesus and out of you will flow rivers of living water (John 7:38).

"Consider the lilies of the field, how they grow"—they simply *are.* Take the sea and the air, the sun, the stars and the moon—they all *are,* and what a ministry they have! So often we mar the influence God designed for us by our self-conscious effort to be consistent and useful. It seems unreasonable to expect a person to consider the lilies, yet that is the only way he or she can grow in grace.

Jesus Christ's argument is that the men and women who are concentrated on their Father in heaven are those who are the fittest to do the work of the world. They have no ulterior motive in arranging their circumstances to produce a fine character. They know it cannot be done in that way. How are you to grow in the knowledge of God? By remaining where you are and by remembering that your Father knows where you are and the circumstances you are in. Keep concentrated on Him and you will grow spiritually as the lily does physically.

"Which of you by worrying can add one cubit to his stature?" Jesus is speaking from the domain of the most basic realities. How many people are born into the world by taking thought? The springs of natural life cannot be reached by the reasoning of common sense, and when you deal with the life of God in your soul, Jesus says in essence, "Remember that your growth in grace does not depend on your watching it, but on your concentration on your Father in heaven."

Notice the difference between the illustrations *we* use in talking of spiritual growth and the illustrations *Jesus* uses. We take our illustrations from engineering enterprises, from automobiles and airplanes and so on, things that compel our attention. Jesus Christ took His illustrations from His Father's handiwork, from sparrows and flowers, things that none of us dream of noticing since we are all breathless and passionate and in a hurry. We may think until we are blue in the face, but Jesus says we cannot add one inch to our height in that way. We cannot possibly develop spiritually in any way other than the way He tells us—by concentration on God.

Our Lord's counsel to His disciples is this: Be as the lily and the star. When we are born from above, we are inclined to become moral policemen, people who unconsciously present ourselves as better than others. We may become intolerable spiritual snobs. Who are the people who influence us most? Those who buttonhole us, or the ones who live their lives as the stars in the heavens and the lilies in the field, perfectly simple and unaffected? These are the lives that mold us—our mothers and wives and friends who are of that order, the order the Holy Spirit produces.

If you want to be of use, get rightly related to Jesus Christ. He will make you of use unconsciously every moment you live. The condition is believing on Him.

## Careful Infidelity • Matthew 6:30–32

Suppose Jesus tells you to do something that is an enormous challenge to your common sense. What are you going to do? Hang back? Once your nerves are in the habit of doing some physical thing, you will do it every time until you deliberately break the habit. The same is true spiritually.

Over and over again, like a runner who won't jump a hurdle, we will get close to what Jesus wants and turn back—until we break that habit and resolutely abandon it. Jesus Christ demands of the person who trusts in Him the same reckless sporting spirit that natural people exhibit in their lives. If someone is going to do anything worthwhile, there are times when he or she has to risk everything on a leap—and in the spiritual world, Jesus Christ demands that we risk everything we hold by our common sense and leap into what He says. As soon as we do, we find that what He says is just as suitable as our common sense.

Following Jesus Christ is a risk, absolutely. We must yield everything to Him, and that is where our infidelity comes in. If we will not trust what we cannot see, if we will not believe what we cannot trace, then our discipleship is at its end. The great word of Jesus to His disciples is *abandon*. When God has brought us into the relationship of disciples, we have to risk everything on His Word. We must trust entirely to Him, and watch that when He brings us to the venture, we take it.

In a person indwelt by the Spirit of God, Jesus sums up commonsense carefulness as infidelity. If, after you have received the Holy Spirit, you try to put other things first instead of God, you will find confusion. The Holy Spirit presses through and says, "Where does God factor in this new relationship? In this planned vacation? In these new books you are buying?" The Holy Spirit always presses that point until we learn to make concentration on God our first consideration. It is not only wrong to worry, it is real infidelity—because it means we do not believe God can look after the little practical details of our lives. It is never anything else that worries us.

Notice what Jesus said would choke the word He puts into us. The Devil? No, the cares of this world. That is how infidelity begins. It is "the little foxes that spoil the vines" (Song of Solomon 2:15), always the little worries. The great cure for infidelity is obedience to the Spirit of God. Refuse to be swamped by the cares of this world, cut out nonessentials and continually revise your relationship to God, and see that you are concentrated absolutely on Him.

People who trust Jesus Christ in a definite practical way are freer than anyone else to work in the world. Free from fret and worry, they can go with absolute certainty into daily life because the responsibility of their lives is not on them, but on God. If once we accept the revelation of Jesus Christ that God is our Father and that we can never think of anything He will forget, worry becomes impossible.

### Concentrated Consecration • Matthew 6:33–34

*"Seek first the kingdom of God and His righteousness,*
*and all these things shall be added to you."*

"Seek first the kingdom of God." We think, "But suppose I do, what about this thing and that? Who is going to look after me? I would like to obey God, but don't ask me to take a step in the dark." We enthrone common sense as almighty God and treat Jesus Christ as a spiritual appendage to it. Jesus Christ hits extremely hard at every one of the institutions on which we naturally bank all our faith. The idea of insurance and property ownership is one of the greatest hindrances to development in the spiritual life. You cannot lay up for a rainy day if you are trusting Jesus Christ.

Our Lord teaches that the one great secret of the spiritual life is concentration on God and His purposes. We talk a lot about consecration, but it ends in sentimentalism because there is nothing definite about it. Consecration ought to mean the definite yielding of ourselves over as saved souls to Jesus and concentrating on that. There are things in actual life that lead to perplexity, and we say, "I am in a quandary and I don't know which way to take." But the apostle Paul says, "Be renewed in the spirit of your mind" (Ephesians 4:23)—concentrate on God, so you may make out what His will is.

Concentration on God is of more value than personal holiness. God can do what He likes with the person who is abandoned to Him. God saves us and sanctifies us, then expects us to concentrate on Him in every circumstance we are in. "I did not immediately confer with flesh and blood" (Galatians 1:16). When in doubt, haul yourself up short and concentrate on God. Every time you do, you will find that God will engineer your circumstances and open the way perfectly—the condition on your part being that you concentrate on God.

"Seek first the kingdom of God and His righteousness, and all these things shall be added to you." In the court of common sense, Jesus Christ's statements are those of a fool—but bring them to the court of faith and the Word of God, and you begin to find, with an awestruck spirit, that they are the words of God.

# Chapter Four

# Character and Conduct
*Matthew 7:1–12*

B ut also for this very reason, giving all diligence, add to your faith virtue. . . ." (2 Peter 1:5). Peter is writing to those who are the children of God, those who have been born from above, and he says, "add, give diligence, concentrate."

*Add* means all that character means. No one is born with character; we make our own character. When we are born from above, a new disposition is given to us but not a new character. We are not born with character either naturally or supernaturally. Character is what we make out of our disposition as it comes in contact with external things.

A person's character cannot be summed up by what he or she does in spots, but only by what the person is in the overall trend of existence. When we describe a man or woman, we fix on the exceptional things—but it is the steady trend of a person's life that tells. Character is that which steadily prevails, not something that occasionally manifests itself.

Character is made by good things done steadily and persistently, not by the exceptional or irregular. The irregular is actually something God mourns over—"your faithfulness is like a morning cloud," He says (Hosea 6:4). In Matthew 7 our Lord is dealing with the need to make character.

## Christian Characteristics
### *(Matthew 7:1–5)*

### The Uncritical Temper • Matthew 7:1
*"Judge not, that you be not judged."*

Criticism is part of the ordinary mental powers of human beings. We have a sense of proportion; we see where things are wrong and we'll often pull the other person to bits. But Jesus says, "As a disciple, cultivate the uncritical temper."

In the spiritual domain, criticism is love turned sour. In a wholesome spiritual life there is no room for criticism. The critical faculty is an intellectual one, not a moral one. If criticism becomes a habit it will destroy the moral energy of life and paralyze the spiritual force. The only person who can criticize human beings is the Holy Spirit. Human beings dare not criticize each other, because as soon as they do, they put themselves in a superior position to the ones they criticize.

A critic must be removed from what he or she criticizes. Before we can criticize a work of art or a piece of music, our information must be complete. We must stand away from what we criticize as superior to it. No human being can ever take that attitude toward another; if we do, we put ourselves in the wrong position and grieve the Holy Spirit.

People who are continually criticized become good for nothing; the effect of the criticism is to knock all the initiative and power out of them. Criticism is deadly in its effect because it divides people's powers and prevents their being a force for anything. That is never the work of the Holy Spirit. The Holy Spirit alone is in the true position of a critic; He is able to show what is wrong without wounding and hurting.

The temper of mind that makes us eagle-eyed in seeing where others are wrong does not do them any good, because the effect of our criticism is to paralyze their powers. That only proves that the criticism was not of the Holy Spirit; we have put ourselves into the position of a superior person. Jesus says a disciple can never stand away from another life and criticize it. So He advocates an uncritical temper: "Judge not." Beware of anything that puts you in the place of the superior person.

The counsel of Jesus is to abstain from judging. At first, this sounds strange because the characteristic of the Holy Spirit in a Christian is to reveal the things that are wrong. But the strangeness is only on the surface. The Holy Spirit does reveal what is wrong in others, but His discernment is never for purposes of criticism—it is for intercession. When the Holy Spirit reveals something of the nature of sin and unbelief in another person, His purpose is not to make us feel the smug satisfaction of a critical spectator—"Well, thank God, I am not like that!" It is to make us take hold of God for that person, so much so that God enables him or her to turn away from the wrong thing.

Never ask God for discernment, because discernment increases your responsibility terrifically. You cannot get out of it by talking, but only by holding up those people in intercession until God puts them right. "If anyone sees his brother sinning a sin which does not lead to death, he will ask, and He will give him life for those who commit sin not leading to death" (1 John 5:16). Our Lord allows no room for criticism in the spiritual life, but He does allow room for discernment and discrimination.

If we let these searchlights go straight down to the root of our spiritual life, we will see why Jesus says, "Don't judge": we won't have time to. Our whole life is to be lived so completely in the power of God that He can pour through us the rivers of living water to others. Some of us are so concerned about the outflow that it dries up. We continually ask, "Am I of any use?" Jesus tells us how to be of use: "He who believes in Me, as the Scripture has said, out of his heart will flow rivers of living water" (John 7:38).

"Judge not, that you be not judged." If we let that maxim of our Lord's sink into our hearts, we will find it brings us to a halt. "Judge not"? Why, we are always doing that! The average Christian is the most penetratingly critical individual—there is nothing of the likeness of Jesus Christ about many of us. A critical temper is a contradiction to all our Lord's teaching. Jesus basically says of criticism, "Apply it to yourself, never to anyone else." Or, as the apostle Paul put it, "Why do you judge your brother? . . . For we shall all stand before the judgment seat of Christ" (Romans 14:10).

Whenever you are in a critical temper, it is impossible to enter into communion with God. Criticism makes you hard and vindictive and cruel, and leaves you with the flattering idea that you are a superior person. It is impossible to develop the characteristics of a saint and maintain a critical attitude. The first thing the Holy Spirit does is to give us a spring-cleaning, and there is no possibility of pride being left in us after that. I never met a person I could despair of after realizing all that lies in *me* apart from the grace of God. Stop having a measuring rod for others. In essence, Jesus says about judging, "*Don't.* Be uncritical in your temper, because in the spiritual domain you can accomplish nothing by criticism."

One of the hardest lessons to learn is to leave the cases we do not understand to God. In every life, there is always one fact more of which we know nothing. So Jesus says, "Judge not." We cannot do that once and assume we are done. We always have to remember that this is our Lord's rule of conduct.

### The Undeviating Test • Matthew 7:2

*"For with what judgment you judge, you will be judged;*
*and with the measure you use, it will be measured back to you."*

This statement of our Lord's is not a haphazard guess—it is an eternal law that works from God's throne right down (see Psalm 18:25–26). The measure you dole out is measured to you again. Jesus speaks of it here in connection with criticism. If you have been shrewd in finding the defects of others, that will be exactly the measure brought back to you— people will judge you in the same way.

"I am perfectly certain that man has been criticizing me," we think. Well, what have you been doing? Life serves back in the coin you pay; you are not necessarily paid back by the same person, but the law holds good: "with what judgment you judge, *you will be judged.*" And it is so with regard to good as well as evil. If you have been generous, you will meet with generosity again; if you dole out criticism and suspicion to others, that is the way you will be treated. There is a difference between repayment and revenge. According to our Lord, the basis of life is repayment, but He allows no room for revenge.

In Romans 2, this principle is applied even more definitely. What if I am guilty myself of what I criticize in another person? Every wrong I see in you, God locates in me; every time I judge you, I condemn myself. "Therefore you are inexcusable, O man, whoever you are who judge, for in whatever you judge another you condemn yourself; for you who judge practice the same things" (Romans 2:1). And God does only not look at the act, He looks at the possibility.

Do we believe the statements of the Bible to begin with? For instance, do we believe that what we criticize in another we are guilty of ourselves? We can always see sin in another person because we ourselves are sinners. The reason we see hypocrisy and fraud and unreality in others is because those sins are all in our own hearts. The great danger is when we call carnal suspicion the conviction of the Holy Spirit. When the Holy Spirit convicts people, He convicts for conversion, that people might be converted and show other good characteristics. We have no right to put ourselves in the place of the superior person and tell others what we see is wrong; that is the work of God's Spirit.

The great characteristic of the saint is humility. We must fully realize that all these sins (and others) would have been shown in our own lives but for the grace of God. Therefore, we have no right to judge. Jesus says, basically, "Don't judge others, because if you do, it will be measured back to you exactly as you have judged."

Which of us would dare stand before God and say, "Lord, judge me as I have judged my fellow humans"? We have often judged other people as sinners; if God had judged *us* like that, we would be in hell. God judges us through the marvelous atonement of Jesus Christ.

### The Undesirable Truth-Teller • Matthew 7:3–5

When it comes to pointing out the defects of others, the "helpful" boldness of the average truth-teller is inspired of the Devil. The Devil is eagle-eyed over things he can criticize, and we are all shrewd in pointing out the speck in our fellow believer's eye. It puts us in a superior position; we believe we are finer spiritual characters than they are.

Where do we find that characteristic? In the Lord Jesus? Never! The Holy Spirit works through saints without their knowledge; He works through them as light. If you do not understand this, you will think your preacher is criticizing you all the time. He is not—it is the Holy Spirit in the preacher discerning the wrong in you.

The last curse in our lives as Christians is the person who becomes a providence to us; he is quite certain we cannot do anything without his advice, and if we do not heed it, we are sure to go wrong. Jesus Christ ridiculed that notion with terrific power: "Hypocrite! First remove the plank from your own eye, and then you will see clearly to remove the speck from your brother's eye." *Hypocrite*—literally, "play actor"—one whose reality is not in keeping with his or her sincerity. Hypocrites consciously play two parts for their own ends. When we find fault with other people we may be quite sincere; yet Jesus says in reality we are frauds.

We cannot get away from the penetrating words of Jesus Christ. If I see the speck in my brother's eye, it is because I have a plank in my own. The statement really hits home. If I have let God, by His mighty grace, remove the plank from my own outlook, I will carry with me the implicit confidence that what God has done for me He can easily do for you—because you have only a splinter, and I had a log of wood! This is the confidence God's salvation gives us. We are so amazed at the way God has altered us that we can despair of no one: "I know God can undertake for you—you are only a little wrong, but I was wrong to the remotest depths of my mind. I was a mean, prejudiced, self-interested, self-seeking person and God has altered me. So I can never despair of you, or of anyone else."

Our Lord's statements save us from the fearful peril of spiritual conceit—"God, I thank You that I am not like other men" (Luke 18:11). They also make us realize why such a man as Daniel bowed his head in vicarious humiliation and intercession—"confessing my sin and the sin of my people" (Daniel 9:20). That call comes every now and again to individuals and to nations.

## Christian Considerateness
*(Matthew 7:6–11)*

Consider how God has dealt with you and then consider that it is for you to do deal likewise with others.

### The Need to Discriminate • Matthew 7:6

*"Do not give what is holy to the dogs; nor cast your pearls before swine, lest they trample them under their feet, and turn and tear you in pieces."*

Jesus Christ is teaching us the need to examine carefully what we present to others in the way of God's truth. If we present the "pearls" of God's revelation to unspiritual people, God says they will trample those pearls under their feet.

Notice He does not say they will trample *us* under their feet (that would not matter so much), but they will trample the truth of God under their feet.

These words are not human words, but the words of Jesus Christ, and the Holy Spirit alone can teach us what they mean. There are some truths that God will not make simple. The only thing God makes plain in the Bible is the way of salvation and sanctification; after that our understanding depends entirely on our walking in the light. Over and over again, people water down the Word of God to suit those who are not spiritual. And so the Word of God is trampled under the feet of "swine."

Ask yourself if you are in any way flinging God's truth to unspiritual swine. "Be careful," Jesus basically says, "not to give God's holy things to 'dogs' (a symbol of the people outside the faith). Don't cast your holy things in front of them, or give the pearls of God's truth to people who are 'swine.'" The apostle Paul mentions the possibility of the pearl of sanctification being dragged into the mire of fornication; it comes through not respecting this mighty caution of our Lord.

We have no right to talk about some points of our experience. There are times of fellowship between Christians when these pearls of precious rarity are turned over and looked at, but if we flaunt them without God's permission to try to convert people, we will find that what Jesus says is true—they will trample them under their feet.

Our Lord never tells us to confess anything but himself: "whoever . . . confesses *Me* before men . . ." (Matthew 10:32). Subjective testimonies to the world are always wrong—they are for saints, for those who are spiritual and who understand. Our testimony to the world must be our Lord Himself. We confess Him, saying, "*He* saved me, *He* sanctified me, *He* put me right with God."

It is always easier to be true to our experience than to Jesus Christ. Many people spurn Jesus Christ in the realm of their particular religious ideas. The central truth is not salvation, or sanctification, or the second coming; the central truth is nothing less than Jesus Christ himself. "I, if I am lifted up from the earth, will draw all peoples to Myself" (John 12:32). Error always comes in when we take something Jesus Christ does and preach it alone as the truth. It is part of the truth, but if we take it to be the whole truth we become advocates of an idea instead of a Person, the Lord himself.

The characteristic of ideas is that they develop an air of finality. If we are only true to a doctrine of Christianity instead of to Jesus Christ, we drive our ideas home with sledgehammer blows. The people who hear us say, "Well, that may be true," but they resent the way our ideas are presented. When we actually follow Jesus Christ, concentrating on Him, the domineering and dictatorial attitudes go away.

### The Notion of Divine Control • Matthew 7:7–10

Always distinguish between being the Spirit's possession and forming the mind of Christ. Here Jesus lays down rules of conduct for those who have the Spirit.

By the simple argument of these verses our Lord urges us to fill our minds with the notion of God's control behind everything—and to maintain an attitude of perfect trust. Settle in your mind the idea that God is there. Once the mind is impressed with that thought, when we are in difficulties it is as easy as breathing to remember, "Why, my Father knows all about it!" It will not be an effort, it will come naturally.

Before, when perplexity pressed upon us, we would go and ask this person or that; now the notion of the divine control is forming so powerfully in us that we simply go to God about it. We will always know whether the notion is working by the way we act in difficult circumstances. Who is the first one we go to? What is the first thing we do? The first power we rely on? This is the working out of the principle indicated in Matthew 6:25–34: God is my Father, He loves me, I can never think of anything He will forget, so why should I worry?

Keep this notion—of the control of God behind all things—strong and growing. Nothing happens in any particular unless God's mind is behind it, so we can rest in perfect confidence. There are times when God will not lift the darkness, but trust Him. Jesus said God will appear at times like an unkind friend (see Luke 11:5–8), but He is not; He will appear like an unnatural father (see Luke 11:9–13), but He is not; He will appear like an unjust judge (see Luke 18:1–8), but He is not. The time will come when everything will be explained. Prayer is not only asking—it is an attitude of heart that produces an atmosphere in which asking is perfectly natural. And Jesus says, "everyone who asks receives."

People will get everything they ask for from life, because they do not ask for anything their will isn't in. If we ask wealth from life, we will get wealth—or we were playing the fool when we asked. "If you abide in Me," Jesus says, "and My words abide in you, you will ask *what you desire,* and it shall be done for you" (John 15:7). Sometimes we pray pious chatter—our will is not in it, and then we say God does not answer. But we never *asked* Him for anything. Asking means that our wills are in what we ask.

You say, "But I asked God to turn my life into a garden of the Lord, and there came the plow of sorrow. Instead of a garden, I have been given a wilderness." Remember that God never gives a wrong answer. Your natural life had to be turned into plowed soil before God could turn it into His own garden. He will put the seed in now. Let God's seasons come over your soul, and before long your life will be a garden of the Lord.

We need to discern that God even controls our asking. We bring in what the apostle Paul calls "will worship" (Colossians 2:23 KJV). Will is the whole individual active; there are terrific forces in the will. The person who gains a moral victory by sheer force of will is the most difficult person to deal with afterwards. The profound thing in people is not sin, but their will. Will is the essential element in God's creation of humans; sin is a perverse disposition which entered into them.

At its basis, the human will is one with God, but it is covered up with all kinds of desires and motives. When we preach Jesus Christ, the Holy Spirit excavates down to the basis of the will and the will turns to God every time. We try to attack people's wills; if we lift up Jesus, He will push straight to the will. When Jesus talked about prayer He never said, "If the human will turns in that direction. . . ." He put it with the grand simplicity of a child—*ask.* We bring in our reasoning faculties and say, "Yes, but . . ." Jesus says, "If you abide in Me, and My words abide in you, you will ask *what you desire,* and it shall be done for you."

### The Necessity for Discernment • Matthew 7:11

*"If you then, being evil, know how to give good gifts to your children, how much more will your Father who is in heaven give good things to those who ask Him!"*

But remember—we have to ask things that are in keeping with the God whom Jesus Christ reveals, things in keeping with His domain. God is not a fortune-teller; He wants to develop in us the character of a child of God. We can know "the things of a man" by "the spirit of the man which is in him," but "the things of God" can only be spiritually discerned (see 1 Corinthians 2:9–14).

The discernment referred to here is the habitual realization that every good thing we have has been given to us by the sheer sovereign grace of God. Jesus says, in essence, "Have this reasoning incorporated into you: how much have you deserved?" The answer is *nothing*—everything has been given to us by God. May God save us from the low, accursed, economical notion that we must only help the people who "deserve it." One can almost hear the Holy Spirit shout in the heart, "Who are you that talk like that? Did *you* deserve the salvation God has given you? Did *you* deserve to be filled with the Holy Spirit?"

Those things are done by the sheer sovereign mercy of God. "Therefore you shall be perfect," Jesus says, "just as your Father in heaven is perfect" (Matthew 5:48). "This is My commandment, that you love one another as I have loved you" (John 15:12). It is not done once and for all; it is a continual, steadfast, growing habit of the life.

Humility and holiness always go together. Whenever hardness and harshness begin to creep into our personal attitude toward others, we may be certain we are swerving from the light. Preaching must be as stern and true as God's Word—never water down God's truth—but when you deal with others, never forget that wherever you stand now, you are a sinner saved by grace. If you stand in the fullness of the blessing of God, you stand there by no other right than the sheer sovereign grace of God.

Over and over again, by our sympathy with them, we blame God for His neglect of people. We may not put it into words, but by our attitude we imply that we are filling up what God has forgotten to do. Never entertain that idea— never allow it to come into your mind. In all probability the Spirit of God will begin to show us that people are where they are because *we* have neglected to do what we ought.

Today the great craze is socialism, and people are saying that Jesus Christ came as a social reformer. Nonsense! We are the social reformers; Jesus Christ came to alter us, and we try to shirk our responsibility by putting our work on Him. Jesus alters us and puts us right; then these principles of His instantly make us social reformers. They begin to work straightway where we live, in our relationships to our fathers and mothers, to our brothers and sisters, our friends, our employers, or employees. "Consider how God has dealt with you," Jesus indicates, "and then consider that you do likewise to others."

# Christian Comprehensiveness

*(Matthew 7:12)*

Christian grace encompasses the whole person. "You shall love the LORD your God with all your *heart,* with all your *soul,* with all your *mind,* and with all your *strength*" (Mark 12:30). Salvation means not only a pure heart, an enlightened mind, and a spirit right with God, but that the whole person is involved in the manifestation of the marvelous power and grace of God. Body, soul, and spirit are brought into a fascinating captivity to the Lord Jesus Christ.

The mantle of a lantern can illustrate the meaning. If the mantle is not rightly adjusted, only one bit of it glows—but when the mantle is adjusted exactly and the light shines, the whole thing is involved in a blaze of light. Similarly, every bit of our being is to be absorbed until we are aglow with the comprehensive goodness of God. "The fruit of the Spirit is in all goodness, righteousness, and truth" (Ephesians 5:9). Some of us have goodness only in spots.

## The Positive Margin of Righteousness

The limit to the manifestation of God's grace in us is our body—the whole of our body. We can understand the need of a pure heart, of a mind rightly adjusted to God, and a spirit indwelt by the Holy Spirit, but what about the body? That is the margin, the outer limit of righteousness in us.

We often divorce the clear intellectual understanding of truth and its practical outcome. Jesus Christ never made such a divorce; He takes no notice of our fine intellectual ideas unless their practical outcome is shown in reality.

There is a great trap in the ability to understand something clearly and then to exhaust its power by stating it. Too much earnestness blinds the spiritual life to reality; earnestness becomes our god. We bank on the earnestness and zeal with which things are said and done, and after a while we find that the reality is not there. The power and presence of God are not being manifested, and when the veneer is scratched in our relationships at home, or in business, or in private, it shows that we are not real.

To say things well is likely to exhaust our power to do those things. So a person often has to curb the verbal expression of a thing and turn it into action. Otherwise, our gift of easy utterance may prevent our doing the things we say.

## The Proverbial Maxim of Reasonableness

*"Therefore, whatever you want men to do to you,*
*do also to them."*

Our Lord's use of this maxim is positive, not negative. *Do* to others whatever you want them to do to you. That's a very different thing from *not* doing to others what you do not want them to do to you. What would we like other people to do to us? "Well," Jesus would say, "do that to them; don't wait for them to do it to you."

The Holy Spirit will stir your imagination to picture many things you would like others to do to you. This is His way of telling you what to do to them. If you think, "I would like people to give me credit for the generous motives I have," give them credit for having generous motives. If you say, "I would like people never to pass harsh judgements on me," don't pass harsh judgments on them. Do you think, "I would like other people to pray for me"? Well, pray for them.

The measure of our growth in grace is our attitude toward other people. "You shall love your neighbor as yourself," Jesus says (Matthew 19:19). Satan comes in as an angel of light (2 Corinthians 11:14) and says, "But you must not think about yourself." The Holy Spirit *will* make you think about yourself, because that is His way of educating you to deal properly with others. The Spirit makes you picture what you would like other people to do to you, and then He says, "Now go and do those things to them."

Matthew 7:12 is our Lord's standard for practical ethical conduct. "Whatever you want men to do to you, do also to them." Never look for right in the other person, but never cease to be right yourself. We always look for justice in this world, but there is no such thing as justice. Jesus essentially says, "Never look for justice, but never cease to give it."

All through our Lord's teaching, the stamp is that of the impossible—unless He can make us all over again, and that is what He came to do. He came to give people a new heredity to which His teaching applies.

## The Principal Meaning of Revelation

Jesus Christ came to make the great laws of God incarnate in human life. That is the miracle of God's grace—we are to be written epistles, "known and read by all men" (2 Corinthians 3:2). There is no allowance whatever in the New Testament for people who say they are saved by grace but do not produce the graceful goods. Jesus Christ by His redemption can bring our actual lives into agreement with our religious profession.

In our study of the Sermon on the Mount it would be like a baptism of light to allow the principles of Jesus Christ to soak right down to our very makeup. His statements are not put up as standards for us to attain; God remakes us and puts His Holy Spirit in us—then the Holy Spirit applies the principles to us and enables us to work them out by His guidance.

# Chapter Five

# Ideas, Ideals, and Actuality
*Matthew 7:13–29*

An *idea* reveals what it does and no more. When you read a book about life, life looks simple; but when you actually face the facts of life, you find they do not align with the simple ideas laid down in the book. An idea is like a searchlight; it lights up what it does and no more, while daylight reveals a hundred and one facts the searchlight had not taken into account. An idea is likely to have an air of finality about it, so we speak of "the tyranny of an idea."

An *ideal* embodies our highest conceptions, but it contains no moral inspiration. To treat the Sermon on the Mount merely as an ideal is misleading. It is not an ideal—it is a statement of the working out of Jesus Christ's disposition in *actuality* in the life of any person. We grow ashamed of not being able to fulfill our ideals, and the more upright we are, the more agonizing our conflict. "I won't lower my ideals," we say, "although I can never hope to make them actual." No one is as frustrated as the people who have ideals they cannot carry out.

Jesus Christ says to such people, "Come to Me . . . and I will give you rest" (Matthew 11:28). Jesus is saying, "I will quiet and calm you, putting something into you that will make the ideal and the actual one." Without Jesus Christ there is an unbridgeable gap between the ideal and the actual; the only way out is a personal relationship to Him. The salvation of God not only saves us from hell, but alters our actual lives.

## Two Gates, Two Ways
### (Matthew 7:13–14)

Our Lord continually used proverbs and sayings that were familiar to His hearers, but He put an altogether new meaning to them. Here He uses an allegory that was familiar in His day, lifting it by His inspiration to embody His patient warnings.

Always distinguish between warning and threatening. God never threatens; the Devil never warns. A warning is God's great, arresting statement, inspired by His love and patience. This throws a flood of light on the vivid statements of Jesus Christ, such as those in Matthew 23. Jesus is stating the inexorable consequence: "How can you escape the condemnation of hell?" (Matthew 23:33). There is no element of personal vindictiveness here. Be careful how you picture our Lord when you read His terrible utterances. Read His denunciations with Calvary in mind.

It is the great, patient love of God that gives the warning. "The way of the unfaithful is hard" (Proverbs 13:15). In your imagination, go behind that statement and see the love of God. He is amazingly tender, but the way of the unfaithful cannot be made easy. God has made it difficult to go wrong, especially for His children.

"Enter by the narrow gate. . . ." If a person tries to enter into salvation in any other way than Jesus Christ's way, he or she will find it a broad way—but the end is distress. The sixteenth-century theologian Erasmus said it took the sharp sword of sorrow, difficulties of every description, heartbreaks and disenchantments to bring him to the place where he saw Jesus Christ as the altogether lovely One. And, he says, "When I got there I found there was no need to have gone the way I went." There is the broad way of reasonable self-realization, but the only way to a personal knowledge of eternal redemption is straight and narrow. Jesus says, "I am the way" (John 14:6).

There is a difference between salvation and discipleship. A man or woman can be saved by God's grace without becoming a disciple of Jesus Christ. Discipleship means a personal dedication of the life to Jesus Christ. People are "saved, yet so as through fire" (1 Corinthians 3:15) who have not been worth anything to God in their actual lives. "Go therefore and *make disciples*" (Matthew 28:19), Jesus said.

The teaching of the Sermon on the Mount produces despair only in a person who is not born again. If Jesus came to be a teacher only, He would have done better to stay away. What is the use of teaching a human being to be what no human being can be—to be continually self-effaced, to do more than his duty, to be completely impartial, to be perfectly devoted to God? If all Jesus Christ came to do was to teach people that, His ideals are the greatest taunts ever presented to the human race. But Jesus Christ came primarily and fundamentally to give new life to women and men. He came to put into any person the disposition that ruled His own life, and as soon as that is given to a person, the teaching of Jesus begins to be possible. All the standards our Lord gives are based on His disposition.

Notice how apparently unsatisfactory Jesus Christ's answers are. He never once answered a question that sprang from a person's head, because those questions are never original—they always have a quibbling note about them. The person with that type of question wants to get the best of it logically. In Luke 13:23–24, a certain devout man asked Jesus a question: "Lord, are there few who are saved?" Jesus replied, "Strive to enter through the narrow gate." That is, Jesus was saying, "See that your own feet are on the right path."

Our Lord's answers seem at first to evade the issue, but He goes underneath the question and solves the real problem. He never answers our shallow questions. Jesus deals with the great unconscious need that makes those questions arise. When people ask original questions out of their own personal lives, Jesus answers every time.

## All Noble Things Are Difficult

Our Lord warns that the devout life of a disciple is not a dream, but a decided discipline which calls for the use of all our powers. No amount of personal determination can give me the new life of God—that is a gift. Where the determination arises is in letting that new life work itself out according to Christ's standard.

We are always in danger of confusing what we *can* do with what we *cannot* do. We cannot save ourselves, or sanctify ourselves, or give ourselves the Holy Spirit; only God can do those things. Confusion continually occurs when we try to do what God alone can do, and try to persuade ourselves that God will do what we alone can do.

We imagine that God is going to make us walk in the light. God will not make that happen; it is *we* who must walk in the light. God gives us the power to do it, but we have to see that we use the power. God puts the power and the life into us and fills us with His Spirit, but we have to work it out. "Work out your own salvation," says Paul (Philippians 2:12). He does not say "work *for* your salvation," but *"work it out."* As we do, we realize that the noble life of a disciple is gloriously difficult—but the difficulty of it rouses us up to overcome, not faint and cave in. It is always necessary to make an effort to be noble.

Jesus Christ never shields a disciple from fulfilling all the requirements of a child of God. Things that are worth doing are never easy. On the ground of redemption, the life of the Son of God is formed in our human nature and we have to "put on the new man" (Colossians 3:10) in accordance with His life—that takes time and discipline. Acquire your soul with patience (see Luke 21:19). "Soul" is my personal spirit manifesting itself in my body—the way I reason and think and look at things. Jesus says that we must lose our souls in order to find them.

We deal with the great, massive aspect of redemption—the idea that God saves by sheer grace through the atonement—but we are apt to forget that it has to be worked out in practical living among other people. "You are My friends,"

Jesus basically says, "so lay down your life for Me. Not to go through the crisis of death, but lay out your life deliberately for Me—take time over it."

It is a noble life and a difficult life. God works in us to do His will, but we must do the doing. Once we start to do what He commands, we find we *can* do it—because we work on the basis of the noble thing God has done for us in redemption.

## My Utmost for His Highest

God demands our utmost in working *out* what He has worked *in*. We can do nothing toward our own redemption, but we must do everything to work it out in actual experience on the basis of regeneration.

Salvation is God's part—it is complete, and we can add nothing to it. But we have to bend all our powers to work out His salvation. It requires discipline to live the life of a disciple in actual things. Jesus "took a towel . . . and began to wash the disciples' feet" (John 13:4–5). It took the incarnate God to do the ordinary, menial things of life rightly—and it takes the life of God in us to use a towel properly. This is redemption actually being worked out in experience, and we can do it every time because of the marvel of God's grace.

"If you love Me, keep My commandments" (John 14:15). Jesus makes this the test of discipleship. The motto over our side of the gate of life is, "All God's commands I can obey." We have to do our utmost as disciples to prove that we appreciate God's utmost for us, and never allow *I can't* to creep in. "Oh, I am not a saint—I can't do that." If that thought comes in, we are a disgrace to Jesus Christ.

God's salvation is a happy thing, but it is also a holy, difficult thing that tests us for all we are worth. Jesus Christ is "bringing many sons to glory" (Hebrews 2:10), and He will not shield us from any of the requirements of sonship. He will say at certain times to the world, the flesh, and the Devil, "Do your worst—I know that He that is in My disciple is greater than he that is in the world" (see 1 John 4:4).

God's grace does not turn out weaklings, but men and women with a strong family likeness to Jesus Christ. Thank God He does give us difficult things to do! Our hearts would burst if there were no way to show our gratitude. "I beseech you therefore, brethren," says Paul, "by the mercies of God, that you present your bodies a *living sacrifice*" (Romans 12:1).

## A Stoot Hairt tae a Stae Brae

*A stoot hairt tae a stae brae*—a strong heart to a difficult hill. The Christian life is a holy life; never substitute the word *happy* for *holy*. We certainly will have happiness, but as a consequence of holiness. Beware of the idea so prevalent today that a Christian must always be happy and bright, to "keep smiling." That is preaching merely the gospel of temperament.

If you make a determination to be happy the basis of your Christian life, your happiness will go from you. Happiness is not a cause, but an effect that follows without striving after it. Our Lord insists that we keep to one point, with our eyes fixed on the narrow gate and the difficult way—which means pure and holy living.

"Take My yoke upon you and learn from Me" (Matthew 11:29). It seems amazingly difficult to put on the yoke of Christ, but as soon as we do, everything becomes easy. In the beginning of the Christian life, it seems easier to drift and to say "I can't." But when we do put on His yoke, we find— blessed be the name of God—that we have chosen the easiest way after all. Happiness and joy appear, but they are not our aim; our aim is the Lord Jesus Christ. Then God showers a hundred times more blessing on us along the way.

To keep a stout heart to the difficult hills of life, watch continually against worry. "Let not your heart be troubled" (John 14:1) is a command, and it means that worrying is sinful. It is not the Devil who switches people off Christ's way, but the ordinary steep difficulties of daily life—difficulties connected with food and clothing and situations. The "cares of this world . . . choke the word" our Lord said (Matthew 13:22).

We all have had times when the little worries of life have choked God's Word, blotted out His face from us, weakened our spirits, and made us sorry and humiliated before Him—this has happened more often than the times we have been tempted to sin. There is something in us that makes us face sinful temptation with vigor and earnestness, but it requires the stout heart that God gives to successfully meet the cares of this life.

I would not give much for the man who had nothing in life to make him say, "I wish I was not in the circumstances I'm in." Jesus said, "In the world you will have tribulation; but be of good cheer, I have overcome the world" (John 16:33). His message for us is this: "You will overcome it too; you will win every time if you bank on your relationship to Me." Spiritual grit is what we need.

"Enter by the narrow gate." We can only get to heaven through Jesus Christ and by no other way. We can only get to the Father through Jesus Christ, and we can only get into the life of a saint in the same way.

## Test Your Teachers
*(Matthew 7:15–20)*

In these verses Jesus tells His disciples to test preachers and teachers by their fruit. There are two tests—one is the fruit in the life of the preacher, and the other is the fruit of the doctrine.

The fruit of a person's own life may be perfectly beautiful, and at the same time he or she may be teaching a doctrine that, if logically worked out, would produce the Devil's fruit in other lives. It is easy to be captivated by a beautiful life and to argue that therefore what the person teaches must be right. But Jesus says, "Be careful—test your teachers by their fruit."

The other side is just as true: a person may be teaching beautiful truths and have magnificent doctrine while the fruit in his or her own life is rotten. We say that if people live a beautiful life, their doctrine must be right; but Jesus says that is not necessarily so. Then again we say because someone teaches the right thing, therefore that person's life must be right; not necessarily so, says Jesus. Test the doctrine by its fruit, and test the teacher by his or her fruit. "Therefore if the Son makes you free, you shall be free indeed" (John 8:36)— the freedom of the nature will work out.

"You will know them by their fruits." You do not gather the vindictive mood from the Holy Spirit; you do not gather the passionately irritable mood from the patience of God; you do not gather the self-indulgent mood and the lust of the flesh in private life from the Spirit of God. God never allows room for any of these moods.

As we study the Sermon on the Mount, we find that the Spirit of God badgers us from every standpoint to bring us into a simplicity of relationship to Jesus Christ. The standard is that of a child depending upon God.

### Possibility of Pretense • Matthew 7:15

*"Beware of false prophets, who come to you in sheep's clothing, but inwardly they are ravenous wolves."*

Our Lord here is describing dangerous teachers, and He warns us of those who come clothed in right doctrine while inwardly their spirit is that of Satan.

It is appallingly easy to pretend. If ever our eyes are off Jesus Christ, pious pretense is sure to follow. The essential condition of the life of the saint is found in 1 John 1:7—"if we walk in the light *as He is in the light*," that is, with nothing folded up and nothing to hide. As soon as we depend upon anything other than our relationship to God, the possibility of pretense comes in. It is a pious pretense rather than hypocrisy. Hypocrites try to live a twofold life for their own ends and succeed. Pious pretense is a desperately sincere effort to be right when we know we are not.

We have to beware of pretense in ourselves. It is an easy business to appear to be what we are not. It is easy to talk and to preach—and to preach our actual life to damnation. It was realizing this that made the apostle Paul say, "I discipline my body . . . lest, when I have preached to others, I myself should become disqualified" (1 Corinthians 9:27).

The easier the expression in words, the less likely is the truth to be carried out in our lives. There is a peril for the preacher that the listener does not have—the peril of expressing a thing and letting the exertion of expression result in never actually doing. That is where fasting has to be exercised—fasting from eloquence, from a fine literary finish, from all that natural culture makes us esteem, if the expression is going to lead us into a limping walk with God.

"This kind can come out by nothing but prayer and fasting" (Mark 9:29). Fasting is much more than doing without food—that is the least part. True fasting is from everything that manifests self-indulgence. In all of us, there is a certain mood which delights in frank speaking, but we may never intend to do what we say. We are, as the Scottish theologian Peter Taylor Forsyth said, "enchanted, but unchanged."

The frank person is the unreliable person, much more so than the subtle, crafty one, because he or she has the power of expressing a thing right out, and there is nothing more to it.

### Place of Patience • Matthew 7:16

*"You will know them by their fruits. Do men gather grapes from thornbushes or figs from thistles?"*

This warning is against overzealousness on the part of heresy-hunters. Our Lord would have us bide our time. Luke 9:53–55 is a case in point. Be careful that you do not allow sinful human suspicion to take the place of the discernment of the Spirit. Fruit and fruit alone is the test. If you see a life's fruit appearing as thistles, Jesus says you will know the wrong root is there—because you do not gather thistles from any root but a thistle root. But remember that it is quite possible in wintertime to mistake a rose tree for something else, unless you are expert in judging.

So there is a place for patience, and our Lord would have us understand this. Wait for the fruit to manifest itself; do not be guided by your own whims. It is easy to get alarmed, persuading ourselves that our particular convictions are the standards of Christ, condemning everyone who does not agree with us to perdition. We feel we must, because our convictions have taken the place of God in us. The Bible never tells us to walk in the light of our convictions, but in the light of the Lord.

Always distinguish between those who object to your way of presenting the gospel and those who object to the gospel itself. There may be many who object to your way of presenting the truth, but that does not necessarily mean that they object to God making them holy. Make room for patience. Wait before passing your verdict. "You will know them by their fruits." If it is given time, wrong teaching produces its fruit just as right teaching does.

### Principle of Performance • Matthew 7:17–18

*"Even so, every good tree bears good fruit, but a bad tree*
*bears bad fruit. A good tree cannot bear bad fruit,*
*nor can a bad tree bear good fruit."*

If we say we are properly related with God, the world has a perfect right to watch our private lives and see if we really are. If we say we are born again, we are put under scrutiny, and rightly so. If the performance of our life is to be steadily holy, the principle of our lives must be holy—that is, if we are going to bring forth good fruit, we must have a good root.

It is possible for an airplane to imitate a bird, just as it is possible for a human being's behavior to imitate the fruit of the Spirit. The vital difference is the same in each: there is no principle of life behind them. The airplane cannot do everything a bird can do; it can only fly as a plane does. If certain conditions keep us from the public gaze, we can get on fairly well with our imitation of the Spirit. But before we can have the true performance in our life, the inside principle must be right—we must know what it is to be born from above, to be sanctified and filled with the Holy Spirit. Then our lives will bring forth fruit.

Fruit is clearly expounded in the New Testament letters, and it is quite different from the gifts of the Spirit or the obvious approval of God for His own Word. It is "the fruit of the Spirit" (Galatians 5:22–23). Fruit-bearing is always mentioned as the manifestation of an intimate union with Jesus Christ (John 15:1–5).

## Power of Publicity • Matthew 7:19–20

> *"Every tree that does not bear good fruit is cut down*
> *and thrown into the fire. Therefore by their fruits*
> *you will know them."*

Jesus Christ makes publicity the test. He lived His own life most publicly (John 18:20). The thing that enraged our Lord's enemies was the public manner in which He did things—His miracles were the public manifestation of His power.

Today people are annoyed at public testimony. But it is no use saying, "Oh, I live a holy life, but I don't say anything about it"—you certainly do not, because the two go together. If something has its root in the heart of God, it will want to be public and get out. It *must* do things in the external and the open. Jesus not only encouraged this publicity, He insisted upon it.

For good or bad, things must be dragged out. "For there is nothing covered that will not be revealed, and hidden that will not be known" (Matthew 10:26). It is God's law that people cannot hide what they really are. If they are His disciples it will be publicly portrayed.

In Matthew 10, Jesus warned His disciples of what would happen when they publicly testified, but His message was basically, "Don't hide your light under a basket for fear of wolfish men. Be careful that you don't go against your duty and have your soul as well as your body destroyed in hell. Be wise as serpents and harmless as doves."

Our Lord warns that the person who will not be conspicuous as His disciple will be made to be conspicuous as His enemy. As surely as God is on His throne, the inevitable principle must work: the revealing of what we really are. God drags everything out in the sun.

The apostle Paul couples sanctification and fornication, meaning that every type of high spiritual emotion that is not worked out on its legitimate level will react on a wrong level. Contact with external elements is necessary to health in the natural world, and the same thing is true spiritually. God's spiritual open air is the Bible.

The Bible is the universe of revelation facts—if we live there, our roots will be healthy and our lives right. It is of no use to say, "I once had an experience." The point is this: Where is it now? Pay attention to the Source, and out of you will flow rivers of living water. It is possible to be so taken up with conscious experience in religious life that we are of no use at all.

## Appearance and Reality
*(Matthew 7:21–23)*

Our Lord makes the test of goodness not only good intentions, but the active carrying out of God's will. Beware of confusing appearance and reality, of judging only by external evidence.

God honors His Word no matter who preaches it. The people Jesus Christ refers to in verse 21 were instruments, but an instrument is not a servant. Servants are those who have given up their right to themselves, to the God they proclaim. They are witnesses to Jesus, a satisfaction to Him wherever they go.

The baptism of the Holy Spirit makes people the incarnation of what they preach, until the appearance and the reality are one and the same. The test of discipleship, as Jesus deals with it in this chapter, is fruit-bearing in godly character—and the disciple is warned not to be blinded by the fact that God honors His Word even when it is preached from the wrong motive (see Philippians 1:15–18).

The Holy Spirit is the one who brings the appearance and the reality together in us. Note that the New Testament never asks us to *believe* the Holy Spirit; it asks us to *receive* Him. He does *in* us what Jesus did *for* us. The mighty redemption of God is made actual in our experience by the living power of the Holy Spirit. He makes the appearance and the reality one and the same thing. He *works in* our salvation and we have to *work it out,* with fear and trembling lest we forget.

Thank God, He does give us the sporting chance, the glorious risk. If we could not disobey God, our obedience would not be worth anything. The sinless-perfection heresy says that when we are saved we *cannot* sin; that is the Devil's lie. When we are saved by God's grace, God puts into us the *possibility* of not sinning, and our character from that moment is of value to God. Before we were saved we had not the power to obey, but now He has planted in us—on the ground of redemption—the heredity of the Son of God. We have the power to obey, and consequently the power to disobey.

The walk of a disciple is gloriously difficult, but gloriously certain. On the ground of the perfect redemption of Jesus Christ, we find that we can begin now to walk worthily—that is, with balance. John the Baptist, "looking at Jesus *as He walked . . .* said, 'Behold the Lamb of God!'" (John 1:36). Walking is the symbol of the ordinary character of a person—no show to keep up, no veneer. "I know that this is a holy man of God, who passes by us regularly" (2 Kings 4:9).

## Recognition of Men • Matthew 7:21

*"Not everyone who says to Me, 'Lord, Lord,'*
*shall enter the kingdom of heaven, but he who does the will*
*of My Father in heaven."*

Human nature is fond of labels, but a label may be the counterfeit of confession. It is so easy to be branded with labels—much easier in certain stages of life to wear a ribbon or a badge than to confess. Jesus never used the word *testify*; He used a much more searching word: *confess.* "Whoever confesses Me before men . . ." (Matthew 10:32). The test of goodness is confession by doing the will of God. "If you do not confess Me before men," Jesus says in essence, "neither will your heavenly Father confess you."

As soon as we confess, we must have a badge; if we do not put one on, others will do it for us. Our Lord is warning that it is possible to wear the label without having the goods; possible for people to wear the badge of being His disciple when they are not. Labels are all right, but if we mistake the label for the goods we are confused.

If we as disciples are to discern between the person with the label and the person with the goods, we must have the spirit of discernment—the Holy Spirit. We start out with the honest belief that the label and the goods must go together. They certainly should, but Jesus warns that sometimes they get severed. And we will even find cases where God honors His Word although those who preach it are not living a right life. In judging the preacher, He says, judge him by his fruit.

### Remedy Mongers • Matthew 7:22

*"Many will say to Me in that day, 'Lord, Lord, have we not prophesied in Your name, cast out demons in Your name, and done many wonders in Your name?'"*

If we are able to cast out demons and do wonderful works, surely we are the servants of God, right? Not at all, says Jesus—our lives must bear evidence in every detail.

In Matthew 7:22, our Lord warns against those who utilize His words and His ways to remedy the evils of humanity, all while being disloyal to Jesus himself. "Have we not prophesied in Your name, cast out demons . . . and done many wonders?"—notice there is not one word of confessing Jesus Christ. They have preached Him as a remedy.

In Luke 10:20, our Lord told the disciples not to rejoice because the demons were subject to them. The disciples should rejoice because they were rightly related to Jesus himself. We are always brought back to this one point—an unsullied relationship to Jesus Christ in every detail, private and public.

### Retributive Measures • Matthew 7:23

> *"And then I will declare to them, 'I never knew you;*
> *depart from Me, you who practice lawlessness!'"*

In these solemn words, Jesus says He will have to say to some Bible expositors, some prophetic students, some workers of miracles, "Depart from me, you who practice lawlessness." These people have twisted the ways of God and made them unequal. "I never knew you," Jesus says, meaning, "You never had my Spirit; you spoke the truth and God honored it, but you were never *of* the truth," And then, the most appallingly isolating and condemning words that could be said to a human soul, "Depart from Me."

Only as we rely upon and recognize the Holy Spirit do we discern how this warning of our Lord's works. We are perplexed because some preach the right thing and God blesses the preaching, and yet all the time the Spirit warns, *No, no, no.* Never trust the best man or woman you ever met; trust the Lord Jesus only. "Lean not on your own understanding" (Proverbs 3:5). "Do not put your trust in princes" (Psalm 146:3). Put your trust in no one but Jesus Christ.

This warning holds good all the way along. If taken as a guide, every character will lead away from God. We are never told to follow in all the footsteps of the saints, but only in so far as they have obeyed God: "who will remind you of my ways *in Christ*" (1 Corinthians 4:17).

Keep right with God; keep in the light. All our anxieties—moral, intellectual, and spiritual—arise on that line. Whenever we take our eyes off Jesus Christ we get startled: "There is another one fallen! I thought he would have stood right." Jesus says, *"Look to Me."*

## The Two Builders

*(Matthew 7:24–29)*

In these verses, our Lord lays the emphasis on *hearing* and *doing.* He has given us His disposition, and He demands that we live as His disciples—now, how are we going to do that? "By hearing My words and doing them," He says.

We hear only what we listen for. Have we listened to what Jesus has to say? Have we paid any attention to finding out what He did say? Most of us do not know what He said. If we have only a smattering of religion, we talk a lot about the Devil; but what hinders us spiritually is not the Devil nearly so much as inattention. We may *hear* the sayings of Jesus Christ, but our wills are left untouched, so we never *do* them. The understanding of the Bible comes only from the indwelling of the Holy Spirit making the universe of the Bible real to us.

### Spiritual Castles • Matthew 7:24

We speak of building castles in the air. That is where a castle should be—whoever heard of a castle underground? The problem is how to get the foundation under your "castle in the air" so that it can stand upon the earth.

The way to put foundations under our castles is by paying attention to the words of Jesus Christ. We may read and listen and not make much of it at the time, but before long we come into circumstances when the Holy Spirit will bring back to us what Jesus said. Now, are we going to obey?

Jesus says that the way to put foundations under spiritual castles is by hearing and doing "these sayings of Mine." Pay attention to His words, and give time to doing it. Try five minutes a day with your Bible. The thing that influences us most is not the thing we give most time to, but the thing that springs from our own personal relationship. That is the prime motive that dominates us.

"You call Me Teacher and Lord, and you say well, for so I am" (John 13:13). But is He? Think of the way we back out of what He says! "I have given you an example, that you should do as I have done to you" (John 13:15). We say it is all very well up to a certain point—and then we abandon it. If we do obey the words of Jesus Christ, we are sure to be called fanatics. Be prepared: the New Testament associates shame with the gospel (see Romans 1:16; 1 Peter 4:12–13).

Our spiritual castles must be conspicuous, and the test of a building is not its fair beauty but its foundations. There are beautiful spiritual structures raised in the shape of books and of lives, full of the finest words and activities—but when the test comes, down they go. They have been built in the air with no foundations, not on the sayings of Jesus Christ.

"Build up your character, bit by bit, by attention to My words," Jesus seems to say. Then, when the supreme crisis comes, you will stand like a rock. The crisis may not come, but if it does, it is all up in about two seconds. There is no possibility of pretense; you are unearthed immediately.

If we have built ourselves up in private by listening to the words of Jesus and obeying them, when the crisis comes it is not our own strength of will that keeps us, but the tremendous power of God—we are "kept by the power of God" (1 Peter 1:5). Go on building yourself up in the Word of God when no one is watching, and when the crisis comes you'll find you will stand like a rock. But if you have not been building yourself up on the Word of God, you will go down, however strong your will.

All you build will end in disaster unless it is built on the sayings of Jesus Christ. But if you are doing what Jesus told you to do, nourishing your soul on His Word, you need not fear the crisis—whatever it is.

### Supreme Catastrophe • Matthew 7:26–27

Every spiritual castle will be tested by a threefold storm: rain, floods, and winds. We can read these as the world, the flesh, and the Devil, and our castles will only stand if they are founded on the sayings of Jesus.

Every spiritual structure built *with* the sayings of Jesus—instead of being founded *on* them—Jesus calls the building of a foolish person. In all of us, there is a tendency to appreciate the sayings of Jesus Christ with our intellects while we refuse to *do* them. If that is the case, then everything we build will go by the board when the test comes.

The apostle Paul applies this in 1 Corinthians 3:12–13, "Now if anyone builds on this foundation with gold, silver, precious stones, wood, hay, straw, each one's work will become clear; for the Day will declare it, because it will be revealed by fire; and the fire will test each one's work, of what sort it is." All has to be tested by the supreme test.

All that we build will be tested supremely, and it will tumble in a fearful disaster unless it is built on the sayings of Jesus Christ. It is easy to build *with* the sayings of Jesus, to sling texts of Scripture together and make them into any kind of structure. But Jesus brings the disciple to the test: "You hear My sayings and quote them, but do you *do* them—in your office, in your home life, in your private life?"

Notice the repulsion you feel toward anyone who tries to build *with* the sayings of Jesus. Our Lord allows no room for having some compartments holy and others unholy. Everything must be radically built *on* the foundation.

## Scriptural Concentration • Matthew 7:28–29

This epilogue is a descriptive note by the Holy Spirit, describing how the people who heard Jesus Christ were impressed by His doctrine. Its application for us is not, "What would Jesus do?" but rather, "What did Jesus say?" As we concentrate on what He said, we can stake our immortal souls upon His words. It is a question not of sentimental consecration but of scriptural concentration.

When Jesus brings something home by His Word, don't shirk it. For example, if you remember something your brother has against you (Matthew 5:23–24), some debt, or some other thing that presses—if you shirk that point, you become a religious fraud. The Holy Spirit's voice is as gentle as a breeze, the merest check; when you hear it, do you say, "But that is only a tiny detail—the Holy Spirit cannot mean that; it is much too trivial"? The Holy Spirit *does* mean that, and at the risk of being thought fanatical, you must obey.

When we are beginning to walk in the right way with God, we will find the spirit of self-vindication will be unearthed. Trying to fulfill what Jesus says will bring it to the light. But what does it matter what anyone thinks of us as long as Jesus Christ thinks we are doing the right thing? What will anything in this life matter as long as we can hear Him say, "Well done, good and faithful servant" (Matthew 25:21)?

# Note to the Reader

The publisher invites you to share your response to the message of this book by writing Discovery House, P.O. Box 3566, Grand Rapids, MI 49501, U.S.A. For information about other Discovery House books, music, or DVDs, contact us at the same address or call 1-800-653-8333. Find us online at dhp.org or send e-mail to books@dhp.org.